LOCOMOTION PAPERS

The
Exeter and Exmouth
Railway

by
Colin G. Maggs

The Esplanade. Exmouth.

THE OAKWOOD PRESS

Originally published as *Railways to Exmouth* in 1980, this substantially revised new edition omits reference to the Budleigh Salterton route to Exmouth which is covered in *The Sidmouth & Budleigh Salterton Branches* (LP193) published in 1996.

British Library Cataloguing in Publication Data
A Record for this book is available from the British Library
ISBN 0 85361 430 X

Typeset by Oakwood Graphics.
Repro by Ford Graphics, Ringwood, Hants.
Printed by Alpha Print (Oxford) Ltd, Witney, Oxon.

Exmouth: train to Sidmouth Junction and Waterloo, *left*; to Exeter Central, *right, c.* 1960.
Lens of Sutton

Title Page: A splendid postcard view of The Esplanade, Exmouth in the early years of the century.

Published by
The Oakwood Press
P.O. Box 13, Usk, Mon., NP5 1YS

Contents

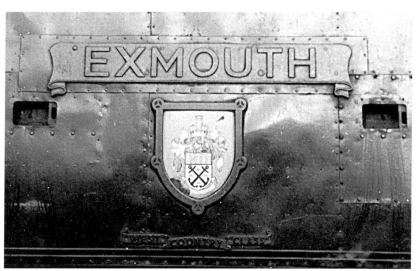

Nameplate of 'West Country' class 4-6-2 No. 34015 *Exmouth*, photographed on 23rd January, 1964. Built in November 1945, it was named at Exmouth on 26th June, 1946. No. 34015 was withdrawn in April 1967 without having been rebuilt.

S.P. Derek

3

PROPOSED
EXETER & EXMOUTH RAIL ROAD.

AT a numerous & highly-respectable MEETING holden at Congdon's Hotel, Exeter, the 28th March, 1825, for the purpose of receiving Mr. CHARLES DEAN's PLAN, REPORT, and ESTIMATE on the proposed EXETER and EXMOUTH RAIL ROAD,

W. H. TONKIN, Esq. in the Chair,

Mr. Charles Dean having read his Report, the following Resolutions were unanimously adopted :—

That a Company be now formed for the purpose of establishing a Rail Road from Exeter to Exmouth; and that it be styled "*The EXETER and EXMOUTH RAIL ROAD COMPANY.*"

That the Capital of this Company be £40,000,— to be raised by Shares of £50 each. And that a Book be forthwith opened for receiving Subscriptions.

That a Provisional Committee, consisting of the following Gentlemen:— *Mr. Tonkin, Mr. Shirley Woolmer, Mr. Lee, Mr. Spettigue, Mr. Staple,* and *Mr. Webber,* be appointed for the purpose of directing Mr. Charles Dean to make a Parliamentary Survey of the proposed Line. And (provided such Committee shall deem it advisable) of obtaining the opinion and report of some eminent Engineer, on such Parliamentary Survey. And that any Three of such Committee be competent to act.

That another General Meeting be called by such Provisional Committee as soon as Mr. Dean shall have completed such Survey, and the Committee are prepared to lay the same before the public.

That Books for Subscriptions be left at the several BANKS in this City, and at EWING's LIBRARY, Exmouth.

That a Deposit of £1. per Share be paid at the time of Subscribing, which Deposit shall be at the disposal of a Provisional Committee for defraying incidental expences.

That at any time within One Month after the next General Meeting shall be held, and Mr. Dean's Parliamentary Survey reported on, it shall be competent for any Subscriber to withdraw his name from the Books of the Company on forfeiting the Deposit.

That the Thanks of the Meeting be given to Messrs. C. Dean and W. H. Furlong, for their exertions in bringing the measure before the public.

That Mr. HENRY CROSS, be the Treasurer.

That Mr. W. H. FURLONG, be the Solicitor.

And that Mr. CHARLES DEAN, be the Engineer.

W. H. TONKIN, *Chairman.*

Resolved,—That the warmest Thanks of this Meeting be given to the Chairman, for his impartial conduct in the Chair.

Advert in *Exeter Flying Post,* 31st March, 1825.

Chapter One

The Exeter & Exmouth Railway
- Birthpangs

The Exmouth branch is an interesting line, being one of the few on the south coast west of Lymington which still features business and holiday traffic in appreciable quantity. It is a commuter line in the best original Southern tradition.

Exmouth, with a population exceeding 32,000, is situated in South-East Devon on the east bank of the River Exe estuary, it is a town with a history. In 1346 the Exe ports supplied Edward III with 10 ships and 193 men for the siege of Calais, but following a decline it could only provide one ship to fight against the Armada. Later, during the Napoleonic wars when the Continent became less accessible for pleasure purposes, Exmouth developed into a watering place. Meanwhile, the Exeter Canal had opened in 1566 and was the first canal for navigation-only ever to be built in England.

In the early 1820s, a group of Exeter businessmen were disturbed by the fact that the size of ships able to use this canal limited access to Exeter. Although James Green had recently carried out dredging and straightening works, it was still inadequate, and so that vessels drawing more water could use it, in 1824 he recommended that the canal should be extended to Turf, two miles further down the west bank of the estuary. Some far-seeing men wondered whether a more economic solution would be to build a quay either at Turf or Exmouth and connect it to Exeter by means of a railroad.

A meeting was held at Exeter on 19th January, 1825 to consider 'the propriety of laying a Rail Road for the more expeditious and economical conveyance of goods from the mouth of the Port of Exeter'. It was resolved 'that such a measure is expedient and will be highly beneficial to the commercial interests of the City and neighbourhood and that it is desirable to call a general meeting of the inhabitants of Exeter and others connected with the Exports and Imports for the purpose of taking their sense in the subject'. Two meetings were held on 27th January: at the Subscription Rooms in the morning and at the Globe Inn in the evening, Sir Digory Forrest, a prominent Exmouth gentleman, being called to the Chair. From the outset of the meeting it was obvious that there was a considerable dissension on the matter of deciding which side of the River Exe the line should run. John Lethbridge outlined the merits of a line on the Exmouth side, estimating the probable costs at about £50,000, and there was talk of forming a dock at Exmouth in conjunction with the proposal to accommodate 40 to 50 ships. James Terrell, an Exeter solicitor, outlined a proposal for running a line along the western bank and terminating at a basin north of Starcross.

J. Glyde summed up the consensus of the meeting by saying that as a merchant frequently engaged in chartering ships from the Continent to Exeter, often he had the greatest difficulty in getting a ship to go to Exeter via the canal and when he did succeed, the fees were at such a premium that it was cheaper for him to ship to Plymouth and haul his goods by road from there, a distance of 43 miles. He said they should not quarrel amongst themselves regarding the best route, but get down to building a railway. The result was that both gatherings resolved: 'That it be desirable that a basin or quay be formed and a Rail Road be laid down for the more easy conveyance of goods from the mouth of the Port of Exeter and Mr Dymond and Mr Lethbridge be requested to make a general survey of the two lines proposed for laying a Rail Road'. The meeting was anxious to waste no time and the matter was adjourned for only seven days in order that the report should be prepared.

John Lethbridge was an architect and Robert Dymond a young engineer and their inexperience in railway matters was criticised by Charles Dean, a civil engineer living at Exeter who had experience of laying railways in Welsh mining valleys. Dean, in a letter to the *Western Luminary* on 1st February, 1825, said he believed that the proposed Bristol & Taunton Railway's extension to Exeter would bring coal and groceries to the city at considerably less expense.

In their report, Lethbridge and Dymond estimated the cost of a railroad from Exeter to Exmouth to be £50,000, while one to Turf would cost £35,000. They considered that the western line, although cheaper, would not be so good for shipping as more navigational hazards were required to be faced. Dean claimed that a railway down the western bank could only produce an annual income of £1,000 whereas an eastern one would bring in £3,000 as the intermediate towns of Topsham and Lympstone would generate more traffic than the villages of Exminster and Starcross on the Powderham side. However, it was resolved, by no means unanimously, to form a company to build a line along the west bank. Its opponents made much of the fact that Lethbridge had, in the space of two weeks, changed his opinion from the Exmouth to the Powderham side and it is quite likely there was a feeling at the time that he had been 'got at'.

The company proposed to raise £35,000 by £25 shares and public notices appeared, but within a week, the champions of the east bank line called a separate meeting and resolved to form a company to put their line to effect, the chief proponent of the scheme being Dean. This company was to raise £40,000 in shares of £50. Reports of the meetings of both companies make fascinating reading, for they pulled few punches and on many occasions individuals came very close to slandering each other. Personalities clashed and reputations suffered, especially those of Lethbridge and Dymond, whose abilities to survey and estimate costings in connection with railways were often questioned. At this point the Exeter Corporation stepped in and promised to extend its canal to Turf to avoid the delays of which there had been so many complaints. For the Corporation, this scheme had the advantage of not robbing Exeter of its trade. Work began on 20th April, 1825 and the expenditure of £113,355 enabled the canal to take vessels of 14 foot draught and about 400 tons burthen. This, of course, put paid to the railway scheme. Both companies had failed to get the necessary backing because railways were a new venture, and this fact may well have prevented the very shrewd Lord Rolle from entering a field in which he would have benefited greatly had the railway succeeded, because in owning half of Exmouth, his property values would have rocketed. Another reason for the railways' failure was that, shortly after the subscription books were laid down, there was a massive rise of 150 per cent in the price of pig iron - a very necessary commodity in railway construction. A ship leaving Newport with a cargo worth £337 docked at Plymouth with its cargo worth £825. A third reason for the failure to build the railway was that a large number of bankruptcies had occurred during the preceding 10 years, making people very wary of speculation.

In 1832 a Turnpike Trust was formed for improving the section of road from Exmouth to Lympstone which met with the Exeter Turnpike Trust road at the top of Lympstone Hill. In 1834 the railway plan was briefly resurrected as part of a scheme to extend the Crediton and Exeter line. The following year there was an application to Parliament by a company proposing a line from Barnstaple to Exmouth with docks at each place, the scheme having the advantage of giving a direct communication from the Bristol to the English Channel.

The summer of 1845 saw Exmouth's railway mania re-starting. On 4th August, the Exeter, Topsham & Exmouth Railway Company issued its Prospectus and only three days later, another company bearing the same name also issued its Prospectus; on neither of the Provisional Committees were there any Exmothians, both being at the instigation of Exeter businessmen. The first of the two companies is generally referred to as 'Daw's company' and the second 'Head's', after the two company secretaries, also local solicitors. Within a short time John Trenchard, a prominent Exmouth solicitor, became associated with the former company and its allocation of provisional shares was going very well. It was not long before several other leading Exmouth gentlemen were elected to the Provisional Committee and a meeting held at the Globe Hotel (situated on the Strand where Clapp's Café existed for many years) endorsed the town's support for Daw's company.

By the end of the year, the Great Western Railway, with its broad gauge of 7 ft 0¼ in., had entered the scene and its supporters proposed floating a company called the Great Western & Exeter, Topsham & Exmouth Junction Railway, hoping to run from St David's station, Exeter. The next development was the South Devon Railway (SDR), another broad gauge company then under construction, proposing to join with Head's company to take the railway to Exmouth by running over SDR metals to the atmospheric pump house north of Exminster, across the Exeter Canal and over the River Exe on a 14 span viaduct to Topsham and so to Exmouth. In spite of Head's company having such a powerful ally as the South Devon, Daw's company pressed on, obtained Board of Trade clearance and entered the tangled web of Parliamentary preliminaries.

The Great Western's line seems to have petered out early in 1846, probably concentrating its support on the line proposed by its ally, but both Head's and Daw's were racing to obtain Parliamentary consent and both stocks were quoted at par on the local stock markets. Both companies' plans were committed after their second reading in the House of Commons in February 1846 and they were running neck and neck. Each party contested the other and both were objected to by Exeter Corporation which was liable to large financial losses on its canal once a railway was in being. It objected to the proposed drawbridge over the canal on the grounds of safety and inconvenience, but Head's company brought out an excellent supporter in the form of the Great

Western's Engineer, I.K. Brunel. He also advocated the adoption of atmospheric traction as on the South Devon Railway, then under construction. To avoid complications it was anticipated that trains would use their momentum to cross the drawbridge. Daw's company objected to atmospheric traction on behalf of Exmouth arguing that the town should not have to tolerate an experimental system.

The outcome was that Head's associates lost the day, the company (wound up in April 1846) returning £1 11s. 6d. of each £2 12s. 6d. deposit paid for each £25 share, so over a period of a year investors lost 40 per cent of their money and had nothing to show for it.

Joseph Locke was the Engineer, and Thomas Whitaker the Residential Engineer, for the longer narrow gauge Daw's scheme, which was to run from Exeter City Gaol to Exmouth all the way along the east bank of the Exe, with a branch leading to Parker's Quay, Topsham. Parliament selected this line as the best for the district and authorised it on 3rd July, 1846, 9 & 10 Vict. cap. 129, under the revised title the 'Exeter & Exmouth Railway' (E&E). It was empowered to raise a capital of £160,000 with borrowing powers of £53,000 and had authority to sell or lease to the London & South Western's Exeter, Yeovil & Dorchester Railway (EY&D).

The company held its first general meeting on 30th July, 1846 when arrangements were made to lease the line to the London & South Western Railway (LSWR). In January 1847 it was proposed that it would be expedient for the E&E to use the EY&D line for approximately a mile between Exeter and Heavitree. An Act, 10 & 11 Vict. cap. 143 of 22nd July, 1847 authorised this and gave the LSWR power to nominate one Director for every 1,300 E&E shares it held, but powers under both Acts were to cease unless the EY&D Bill received sanction in 1846 or 1847. It was not passed until 22nd July, 1848 (11 & 12 Vict. cap. 85) so the E&E applied for and received an extension of time for three years, 11 & 12 Vict. cap. 157, 31st August, 1848. Because of the shortage of money following the aftermath of the Railway Mania, the EY&D was abandoned and with it, the last forlorn hope of the E&E which depended on the LSWR lease. The failure to build the line rather embarrassed an enterprising Exmouth hotelier who had already named his premises the Railway and Commercial - it stood on the Strand where Hancock & Wheeler the ironmongers are today.

In May 1850 the Directors considered abandoning the E&E and on 10th June, 1851 a special meeting was held to determine whether the railway should continue. The meeting could not be held because so little interest was shown that not even a quorum of shareholders put in an appearance.

The LSWR offered only 10 shillings a share for which shareholders had been required to pay a deposit of 21 shillings to cover the heavy Parliamentary expenses due to the opposition of the broad gauge party. In 1851 two local companies made unsuccessful attempts at reviving interest in a railway to Exmouth. In the autumn, Robert Wreford, yet another Exeter solicitor who entered the scene, re-proposed the broad gauge Exminster to Exmouth line, while Daw revived the narrow gauge scheme for connecting Exmouth with the proposed Exeter to Yeovil line. A large and influential meeting was held on 15th December, 1851 in Bastin's Globe Hotel, Exmouth, to establish which of the two lines the town preferred. Although the scales came down on the side of the narrow gauge line, Exmouth was prepared to support any promoter who would give it rail communication. In the autumn of 1852 Wreford revised his ideas and proposed an alternative broad gauge line with W.R. Neale as Engineer, this time running down the east bank of the river from Exeter to Exmouth. The proposal was supported by Daniel Warren, an Exmouth solicitor, who imaginatively suggested that the railway should run from The Point, Exmouth, to Lympstone on an embankment which would enclose hundreds of acres of valuable land and reclaim it from the sea. Others did not view the scheme with such optimism, but it was put forward again the following year with the addition of a branch to Topsham quay, again without success.

In December 1853 the E&E Prospectus appeared proposing to raise £160,000 in £20 shares for Daw's narrow gauge scheme. John Henry Walker, later squire of Marpool Hall, Exmouth, was elected Chairman of the E&E Provisional Committee. As much information had already been gathered as a result of previous efforts, a promise was made to shareholders that no more than 10 shillings per share would be spent on Parliamentary expenses. This project captured the interest of the town and there was a crowded meeting despite heavy snow and by January 1854 Exmouth had promises of £15,000 of the £20,000 the town had indicated it could raise. In 1854 Wreford and Brunel made another sortie for crossing the canal and river from the broad gauge line at Exminster, and Exmouth inhabitants, thinking that the LSWR had deserted them since it had made no moves, transferred their support to the broad gauge proposal. It was a similar scheme to that put forward in 1846, but with the addition of a separate line from the SDR to Exeter quay and with the estimate dramatically reduced to £70,000. There was also talk of a contractor who was prepared to undertake construction and take leasing rights as part payment for his services.

Whilst being cross-examined about the scheme in the House of Commons Committee, its engineer was asked, 'Pray, Mr Brunel, did you ever know Parliament sanction a bridge over a tidal river which bridge compelled vessels to lower their mast?'

'Yes', replied the civil engineer, 'I rather think I do'.

'Have the goodness to tell me where it is?'

'Why, here, close to this House, and if you will step to the window I will show it to you'.

His cross-examiner dropped the subject without going to the window and looking at Hungerford Bridge.

On 2nd July, 1855 by 18 & 19 Vict. cap. 122, the Exeter & Exmouth Railway Company's Bill was passed by Parliament. This authorised Wreford and Brunel's broad gauge line via Exminster and Topsham. The City of Exeter had unsuccessfully opposed the Bill, not on account of the broad gauge, but because of insufficient height to the bridge over the canal and the fact that trains would have had precedence at the bridge and a delay in opening could have led to a ship losing a tide. Sir John Duckworth of Nutwell Court, north of Lympstone, the one objecting landowner, was adequately compensated, part of the atonement being that the telegraph wires were placed underground so as not to obscure the view from his house. The Rolle Trustees who were managing the Estate until the late Lord Rolle's heir came of age, petitioned the Court of Chancery for permission to lend money to the E&E, to be converted into shares on the attainment of the Hon. Mark Rolle's majority in 18 months' time. In 1855 pressure was put on the LSWR by the legislature for constructing a narrow gauge Yeovil to Exeter line, but at this stage, it seemed too late to alter the route of the E&E.

By 24th April, 1856 £13,810 had been subscribed at Exmouth, £9,280 at Exeter, £1,100 at Topsham, £1,093 at Budleigh Salterton with sums from other places making a total of £31,180, but the Directors wanted £40,000 before placing the contract. In fact there was almost an impasse because potential investors were waiting for a sound financial position and this could not materialise until investors came forward, but by September the necessary sum had been subscribed and the Directors commenced buying land.

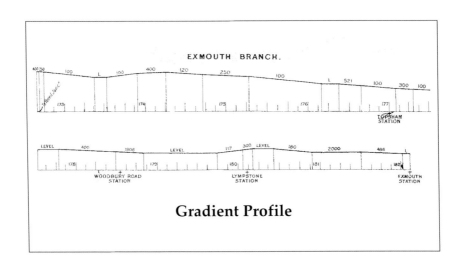

Gradient Profile

Chapter Two

Construction Begins

The ceremony of turning the first sod took place at the site of Exmouth station on 27th November, 1856. It was a day of dual festivities as it coincided with celebrations for the Hon. Mark Rolle who had attained his majority earlier that month. He was two hours late in arriving at Exmouth and when he did arrive it was supposed that either he was dying of hunger, or else too overcome to undertake turning the first sod, for as the Directors passed by the Market House where the feast was to be held, instead of going on to turn the turf first, he alighted and left the procession. The sod-turning ceremony was eventually carried out by the company's Chairman, John Walker.

In lifting the turf he snapped the handle of the spade. Not to be outdone, he lifted the sod with his hands, dropped it into the mahogany wheelbarrow and wheeled it off to another spot where he tipped it out on to the ground. Fortunately these mishaps were not an immediate ill omen for the breakdown of the company, as within a week or so Captain McNair, on behalf of Brunel, was busily engaged in marking out the line between Exmouth and the River Clyst near Topsham. However there were murmurings at a meeting in September 1857 when E&E shareholders began to turn publicly on their Directors. Sheppard, an Exmouth shipowner, postmaster and auctioneer, appealed for a vote of confidence in himself as he had been responsible for negotiating the terms offered by the South Devon Railway and rejected by the E&E.

Immediately this vote was given, Mr Pratt and Dr Spettigue, both prominent Exmouth businessmen, resigned their Directorships. The Chairman and the rest of the Directors said that they hoped the two men would reconsider their decision, otherwise they said that they too would resign and leave Sheppard as the sole Director. Sheppard's fellow Directors felt particularly bitter towards him as he had not paid his share call. Why he had not done so was subsequently made clear on 23rd November, 1858 when a petition for bankruptcy was filed against him. His downfall was not primarily due to his railway interests, but more to his shipping reversals, but of course, the railway situation did not help him.

On 1st August, 1857 the Directors reported that they had arranged with the Bristol & Exeter Railway (B&E) and SDR to lease the line (but not the branch to the quay at Exeter), for 10 years at £3,000 annually, plus four per cent on the capital expenditure on stations and 20 per cent of the gross annual receipts exceeding £6,000. Far from showing approbation for this step, the shareholders appointed a committee whose report rejected the agreement, preferring the LSWR line after all and ordering a start on earthworks between Exmouth and Topsham. They were intent on lowering the costs of the railway, which, exclusive of the Exmouth Quay line, were estimated to be £94, 435.

Ritson, the contractor, offered a price in excess of the £30,000 likely cost suggested by the E&E company's Engineer in 1856, as he agreed to accept shares instead of cash and was therefore taking a bigger risk. The committee proposed reducing the cost by offering him cash instead of shares. To do this it was necessary to ask for an immediate subscription of £12,000, but this appeal failed. The committee had greater success with regard to the lease, for in September 1857 the Yeovil & Exeter Railway resolved to make a branch line from Exeter to Topsham, with the Exmouth company continuing the railway from Topsham to Exmouth. The completed line was to be worked by the LSWR for 50 per cent of the gross receipts, the sum to be determined by respective mileage of 5 miles 31 chains to the LSWR and 5 miles 43 chains to the E&E. This proposal was certainly advantageous as the local company avoided having to foot the bill for the expensive bridging over the Exeter Canal and the River Exe. The two companies were to share the cost of building Topsham station and the branch down to the quay. This alteration meant that a new Act had to be sought for powers to abandon part of the authorised line; to make new works and to reduce the capital from £70,000 to £50,000 and borrowing powers from £33,000 to £16,000. This was granted in 21 & 22 Vict. cap. 56 of 28th June, 1858, the LSWR receiving powers to make a branch to Topsham on 12th July, 1858.

J.E. Errington was appointed Engineer, with W.R. Galbraith as Residential Engineer. Bridges and stations were to the designs of Sir William Tite, LSWR Architect and one of the top four of the time. As well as designing stations for his company he was responsible for some on the Caledonian Railway and also on the Le Havre to Paris line.

The E&E general meeting on 31st August, 1858 became rowdy when the enthusiastic supporter of the broad gauge, excitable Robert Wreford, was not allowed to address the meeting. Wreford threatened to horsewhip the Chairman, who then called him a 'confounded blackguard'. (The Chairman was J.H. Walker Aylesbury who, since the turf cutting ceremony had taken place, had benefited from a legacy, taking the title 'Aylesbury' as a condition.) Wreford was upset because he had spent £1,290 out of his own pocket on the Exmouth Railway and had received no return.

Tenders for the construction of the line were requested in January 1859 and by March a contract was signed with James Taylor of Northernhay, Exeter, for building the Topsham to Exmouth line at a cost of £39,000 which excluded stations and the telegraph. Taylor was to take £10,000 in shares and have the line ready for traffic by 1st May, 1860. Taylor converted some of the clay from the cuttings into bricks for bridges and culverts and by August 1859 had started on cofferdams for the River Clyst Viaduct. This was the only engineering difficulty encountered; owing to the shifting and insubstantial nature of the river bed, the foundations for the piers had to be taken down to a depth of 25 feet. Heavy storms in the early weeks of 1860 prevented supplies of stone for the viaduct, bridges and culverts being brought by sea from Babbacombe, near Torquay and in August this was still the excuse for the late delivery of stone, but two out of the five miles of line had been completed. A violent storm that month washed away hundreds of tons of ballast, but stations were being built, 500 men and 50 horses were at work and from September a locomotive was used. Taylor said that if he had five weeks of fine weather the line would be opened by 1st December. On 13th October the Directors made a trip on the contractor's engine at Lympstone.

Chapter Three

Opening and Subsequent History

Thirty-six years after the first proposal had been made, the line was eventually completed. Colonel William Yolland inspected it on behalf of the Board of Trade on 27th April, 1861, the train consisting of two tender engines, two coaches and a brake van. The locomotives were well-coaled to give plenty of weight for bridge testing. He wrote the following reports:*

Stoke near Devonport
27th April, 1861

Sir,

I have the honor [*sic*] to report for the information of the Lords of the Committee of Privy Council of Trade, that in obedience to your minute of the 20th Instant, I have this day inspected the Topsham Branch of the London and South Western Railway which forms a junction with the main line of the Yeovil and Exeter Section of the L&SWR at about a mile from Exeter, and which ends at Topsham, a length of 4 miles and 35 chains.

This Branch is single with the exception of a short length at the Junction, and of a loop siding at the only station on the Line at Topsham, but the land has been purchased and the Bridges have been constructed for a double line of Railway, if hereafter required.

The width of the Line at formation level is 10 feet - the gauge 4 ft 8½ in. and the width of the Line where double or at sidings, is 6 feet.

The line is laid with double headed rails weighing 75 lbs per linear yard in lengths of 21 feet. The joints are fished with Adams' wrought iron Bracket chairs, which are bolted to the rails by four wrought-iron bolts, and spiked down to the transverse sleepers by two spikes. Each Bracket is 15 inches long and weighs about 20 lbs. The Intermediate Chairs each weigh about 23 lbs and they are spiked to the transverse sleepers by two ¾ inch spikes, six inches long and the rails are held in the chairs by oak keys six inches in length.

The sleepers are mostly of Memel timber creosoted, but a small proportion of Larch not creosoted have been used. They are 9 feet long and 10 inches wide by 5 inches deep - the Joint-sleepers being rectangular while the intermediates are half round. They are placed transversely 3 ft 2 in. apart, centre to centre, next [to] the joints and the remainder are 3 ft 8 in. apart, centre to centre.

The Ballast is of sand, broken stone and gravel, laid it is stated, 2 feet deep under the surface of the rail and 11 feet wide at the surface and 15 feet at formation level.

There are six under and two over bridges. The largest span of the under bridges is 30 feet on the square and 46⅔ feet on the skew - and of the overbridges 30 feet on the square and 34⅔ feet on the skew. Three of the under bridges have cast-iron girder tops resting on Brick or stone abutments and the remainder of the Bridges are built either of Brickwork or with Brick and Mortar and Stone Quoins. The Girder bridges are sufficiently strong, and the Brickwork is well executed and sufficiently strong. There are no unauthorised Level Crossings on the Line.

No engine Turntable has been provided on this Branch, but one is fixed at the Exmouth Terminus of the Exeter and Exmouth Railway which is a direct continuation of this Branch Line, and which is to be worked in connection with the same by the London and South Western Railway.

Indicators are to be attached to work in connection with the facing Points on the Line. The Resident Engineer has promised to attend to this small requirement.

* PRO Kew MT6/23/26 and MT6/23/27.

13

Arrival of a double-headed train at Exmouth station on the opening day, 1st May, 1861.
Courtesy Illustrated London News

The exterior of Exmouth station, *c.* 1861.   *Author's Collection*

I have not received any undertaking as to the mode of working this single line, but I understand that one will be sent to the Board of Trade, and that the line is to be worked by a single Engine.

The line has been very well finished off and is in good order.

I have therefore to report that I am of [the] opinion that their Lordships sanction for the opening of the Topsham Branch of the London and South Western Ry for Public Traffic may be given, as soon as the undertaking to which I have referred is received.

I have the honor to be,
Sir,
Your most obedient Servant
W. Yolland (Colonel)
Royal Engineers

Stoke near Devonport
27th April, 1861

Sir,

I have the honor to report for the information of the Lords of the Committee of the Privy Council for Trade, in obedience to your minute of the 16th Instant, that I have this day inspected the Exeter and Exmouth Railway which is a continuation of the Topsham Branch of the London & South Western Railway from Topsham to Exmouth, a length of 4 miles and 77 chains. [sic]

This Line is single, with the exception of a short length at the Junction with the Topsham Branch and of short lengths at two Stations on the Line, Lympstone and Exmouth. There is no Siding at the remaining Station at Woodbury Road. But the land has been purchased, and the Clyst Viaduct and the Bridge at 2m 74¾ chains [Lympstone Viaduct. Author] and all over bridges have been constructed for a double Line of Railway - but the remaining bridges are only built for a single Line.

The permanent way is precisely similar to that laid on the Topsham Branch of the London and South Western Railway and described in my report of Inspection of this date.

There are two over and 10 under Bridges with two Viaducts.

The longest span of the two overbridges is 30 feet on the square and 34⅔ feet on the skew. They are both built of Brick in Mortar. The longest span of the underbridges is 30 feet on the square and 30¼ feet on the skew. Five of the under bridges are built either entirely of Brick or with Brick and Stone Quoins - two have Brick or Stone abutments and cast-iron Girders and three have Brick or Stone abutments and Timber beams - these last are all of small span.

Of the Viaducts that of the Clyst has five openings averaging about 60 feet span and the other at the Boat Docks, three are two openings of 24½ feet and one of 13¼. The piers and abutments are built of stone. The Clyst Viaduct has wrought iron continuous girders and the Boat Dock Viaduct cast-iron Girders. The second Line of Railway is not laid over the two Viaducts, so that the central girder of the Clyst Viaduct has not been tested. The Masonry and Brickwork in the Bridges and Viaducts are well executed and the iron and wood superstructures are well put together and sufficiently strong.

There are no unauthorised Level Crossings on the line.

Indicators are to be attached to facing Points, and there is still a short length of pitching of the Sea Wall which remains to be done - but it is completed to above the Level of High water.

An Engine Turntable has been erected at the Exmouth Station.

I have not received the undertaking as to the mode of working the line, which is to be performed by the London & South Western Railway in connection with their Topsham Branch - but I understand it is to be sent to the Board of Trade, and to be done by a single

Engine in steam.

I have now therefore to report that the opening of the Exeter and Exmouth Railway for Public Traffic may be sanctioned by their Lordships as soon as this undertaking has been received.

I have (etc.)

W. Yolland (Colonel)

Royal Engineers

The Reverend J.T. Rocke, Vicar of Holy Trinity Church, Exmouth, was elected Chairman of the committee set up to arrange the opening celebrations which were to include decorations, a procession and a banquet. The opening day, 1st May, 1861, was declared a general holiday in the town. The Exeter *Flying Post* enthusiastically reported:

May Day, 1861, will for the future rank as one of the brightest of Red Letter Days in the annals of Exmouth. It is the day on which the long-deferred hope of the principal of its inhabitants has at last been realised - the day on which, after more than sixteen years' patience and struggling with a series of rare difficulties - difficulties such as few lines have had to contend against - the wild expectations of 1845 have been consummated. This afternoon Exmouth has been formally brought into the only direct communication with this city and the metropolis, and of course inferentially with everywhere else - recognised in this age of railways; and the accomplishment of this project has been commemorated with demonstrations corresponding to the importance of the event to those immediately concerned. In other words the opening of the Exeter and Exmouth line of railway has taken place this afternoon with all the *éclat* which could be given to such an event by fine weather - a most material point in things of this description - by popular processions, by the cheering of enthusiastic crowds of sightseers, by bell-ringing, brass bands, banquets, speeches, bunting, and the florist's art.

The first train consisting of 11 coaches and carrying about 150 passengers left Exeter Queen Street at 7.46 am drawn by a 2-2-2 well tank locomotive No. 36 *Comet* decorated with flags. It arrived at Exmouth 30 minutes later at 8.16.

The second train was announced to start from the Exeter station at 10.45, and long before that time the platform was crowded with passengers eagerly desirous of obtaining places. Within five or six minutes of the specified time the train, which numbered seventeen or eighteen carriages, and headed by two locomotives, started to the dismay of some hundreds, who evidently, not expecting so sudden a departure, had not taken their places - no doubt partly owing to the difficulty in finding places to take. Be that as it may, a vast concourse were left behind on the platform, and these were relieved with the information that there would be another train in a short time to forward them.

Topsham was decorated.

At Lympstone the display was on a scale infinitely surpassing what might have been expected even of a village which on previous occasions has shown that it is possessed of a public spirit only equalled - if indeed it may be said to be equalled - by Exmouth itself . . . The inhabitants of Lympstone and the neighbourhood came forward most liberally and a sum amounting to upwards of £30 was collected . . . the Railway Hotel, erst by the by the Swan - promptly changed its name with the changed circumstances . . . Mr Hallett, Mr Marshall, and Mr Long erected triumphal arches, and several of the other principal inhabitants displayed flags from their houses.

At twelve a procession in the following order was formed and paraded the village:- A banner bearing the inscription, 'Prosperity to the Exeter and Exmouth Railway'; a brass band; a detachment of the Lympstone members of the Exmouth Rifle Corps; and a body of the Coast Guard Preventive Service, preceded by a flag inscribed in honour of the Army and Navy and Volunteers. This martial portion of the procession was followed by representatives of trade and commerce carrying their banner, by 'Britannia' and 'Neptune', each with their satellites; and was closed by the children of the village dressed in white, including the children attending National Schools . . . These children carried a variety of flags.

After marching through the village, the procession proceeded to the Cliff Field, kindly lent for the occasion by Mr Bennett. Over the entrance to this field, spanned by a triumphal arch, hung a banner with the following lines:

Young and old come forth and sing,
Children join the jocund ring,
Striplings blythe and maidens gay
Hail the Railway Holiday!

Having marched round the field, which was thronged by a considerable number of visitors, the procession sat down to an excellent cold collation of roast beef and plum pudding. At the conclusion of the repast the party joined in games, and in this way the remainder of the afternoon was passed.

It was originally arranged that the directors of the line and officers should have proceeded by the second train; but a telegraph having been received to the effect that the Exmouthonians were not prepared for their reception, it was resolved to start a special train at twelve o'clock.

The 10.45 train proceeded at a medium rate, and in about a quarter of an hour reached Topsham, having passed through a fine track [sic] of country, which afforded some excellent and extensive views, for which this line will become noted, on each side of Topsham. Arriving at Topsham station, which has a very picturesque appearance, the platform was found to be crowded with would-be passengers; but many of these had to submit to a similar ordeal as those of their Exeter friends - no room being found to accommodate them . . . The train arrived at Exmouth at half-past eleven.

The Exeter Artillery Company journeyed to Exmouth in this train, and the excellent fife and drum band of the corps played some lively and spirited tunes at each station.

On arriving at Exmouth the various volunteer corps - the Exeter, Topsham and Woodbury Artillery Companies, and the Topsham and Exmouth Rifle Companies (the latter of which we regret to say only number a few men) - were drawn up in line, and headed by the Exmouth band marched from the station.

As might be expected, the inhabitants of Exmouth appeared determined to celebrate the opening of this line, which put them in direct communication with London, with every manifestation of gaiety and joy. Probably, not within the recollection of the 'oldest inhabitant', has there been so vast a concourse of people as were witnessed in Exmouth today. From nearly every house flags - with and without mottoes - were suspended, and fir trees were planted in the principal streets and around the market. On leaving the station the first decoration of importance that met the eye of the visitor was a triumphal arch, erected across the Strand, festooned with evergreens and flags, bearing the mottoes of 'Success to the Iron Road', and 'Time is Money'. At the junction of the Strand, with Albion-street, Chapple-street and the Exeter-road, was another arch similarly decorated with flags, &c., and the appropriate mottoes 'Agriculture and Commerce', 'Peace and Plenty', and 'God Save the Queen'. At Webber's Corner, leading to Chapple-hill, the most picturesque arch was erected, beautifully ornamented with flowers, flags, &c. This arch was erected at the cross-roads, facing each was a flag bearing different mottoes. Thus, facing the Strand, was a flag with the motto 'Prosperity and Commerce', on the inverse, 'May our Hopes be Realized'. Facing the road leading from the beach was inscribed on a flag 'Excursion for the Million', and the fourth flag bore the motto of 'Increase of Trade'. Flags were suspended from houses on the Beacon, and here also was a triumphal arch, with the usual appurtenances. On the principal flags were inscribed 'Our Gallant Volunteers', and 'Welcome to Visitors'.

Very shortly after one o'clock the directors train, [16 coaches and piloted. *Author*] which brought with it the passengers who were left behind from the former train, arrived at the Exmouth station.*

At 3.00 pm a banquet was held in the Globe Hotel, Exmouth, an event which proved to be more memorable than most opening dinners since among the guests was the American George Francis Train (of tramway fame) who had opened two lines in London during the previous four weeks. A good speaker, he received applause and laughter when he remarked that 'though you have built your houses on the sands, you have founded your church upon a Rocke' and 'but for the kind invitation I received from Mr Dutton [the Hon. Ralph H. Dutton, an LSWR Director], you would have had today one Train the less'.

A later speaker was Sergeant Gaselee who proposed a toast to the press, but then went on in political vein to advocate free trade, his speech arousing a clamour of dissension. Wreford stood on a bench to support his friend Gaselee and was pelted with orange peel by Mr Bickle. After a sharp tussle, Wreford was overpowered and expelled struggling and triumphantly waving Bickle's cravat. Lieutenant Adams, in the Chair remarked: 'Hitherto I have had great pleasure in presiding over you; but upon my word if I have a continuance of the row and cabal which has been displayed in this room during the last ten minutes, I can no longer act with pleasure'.†

During the first five days, the line was used by an average of more than 2,000 passengers a day and the number of tickets issued to 31st August, 1861 was 80,000. Up to 26th February, 1862 the total receipts from Exmouth were £4,726 11s. 3d. and goods £553 19s. 6d., with net takings of £3,563 11s. 3d. giving the Exmouth company £1,207 12s. 8d., but no dividend was declared. From the opening of the line, the LSWR let by the year the refreshment room and dwelling house attached to Exmouth station. The railway plant used in the construction of the Topsham to Exmouth section was auctioned at Topsham on 3rd June, 1861. An Act 24 & 25 Vict. cap. 15 of 17th May, 1861 authorised the E&E to raise an additional capital to the extent of £30,000 in five per cent shares; to cancel forfeited shares and to re-issue others in lieu. In June 1862 Woodbury Road station was still unfinished as trouble was being encountered with efflorescence from the brickwork rendering the decorations hopeless, while similar trouble was experienced in the waiting room at Exmouth.

At the half-yearly meeting on 27th February, 1863, the proprietors, peeved at receiving only a fraction of the expected dividend, called the original shareholders an unfortunate and disillusioned body', blaming J.H. Walker Aylesbury, their past Chairman, for the 'disastrous agreement' by which the LSWR worked the line and unsuccessfully demanded that the LSWR should

---

* *Flying Post*, 1st May, 1861.
† *Woolmer's Exeter & Plymouth Gazette*, 3rd May, 1861.

reduce its charge from 50 to 40 per cent of the gross receipts.

This meeting also rescinded a resolution passed on 29th August, 1859 which stated that compensation for Wreford would be deferred until the original shareholders were paid a dividend of three per cent. A poll taken on 7th October, 1863 was against him being given any compensation whatsoever. His failure to promote the E&E reflected badly in the support he was given for the Ilfracombe Railway - another of his interests. Regarding the E&E, Wreford appears to be an eccentric character, but his efforts with the Ilfracombe Railway seem quite rational. (See *The Barnstaple and Ilfracombe Railway* by the present author, published by The Oakwood Press.) At a meeting of the E&E on 26th August, 1864 he asserted that a falsehood had been inserted in the company's books, and he would not recognise Dr Brent as Chairman. Wreford died on 10th November, 1864, it being believed that the trouble he experienced with the E&E and his numerous efforts to obtain redress in the matter contributed strongly towards his death.

On 1st November, 1864 a meeting was held to consider amalgamation with the LSWR and the proposal received almost unanimous assent. The necessary Act authorising this was passed on 5th July, 1865, 28 & 29 Vict. cap. 304. The amalgamation took place on 1st January, 1866.

In 1864 the E&E's capital and borrowing power and debenture debt was as follows:

		£
Capital authorised		80,000
Capital raised		
£5 per cent preference capital	£27,000	
Ordinary capital	£36,800	63,800
Capital not raised		16,200
Borrowing power		16,600
Debenture debt		16,600

After amalgamation the LSWR was required to create and issue £27,000 £4 10s. preference stock in exchange for £27,000 E&E 5 per cent stock and create and issue to the holders of £36,800 Exmouth ordinary stock, £18,400 of LSWR stock, either ordinary or 4½ per cent preference.

The Exmouth & Salterton Railway opened on 1st June, 1903 bringing more traffic to Exmouth and enabling through coaches from Waterloo to be detached at Sidmouth Junction and travel by a more direct route instead of via Exeter. This line closed on 6th March, 1967. The full story of the Budleigh Salterton and Sidmouth lines can be found in a companion book in the series (LP193).

The LSWR opened Lion's Holt and Mount Pleasant Road halts on 26th January, 1906 with the inauguration of Exeter's first rail-motor service to Honiton. On 31st May, 1908 track was doubled between Exmouth Junction and Topsham at a cost of some £16,000 and further halts were opened on this date at Polsloe Bridge and Clyst St Mary & Digby served by a new Exeter-Topsham 'motor' service. Doubling the line involved a new siding being laid with scissors crossover from the up line to the Exeter Brick & Tile Company's works,

Exmouth station *c.* 1861.   *Author's Collection*

Exterior of Exmouth station, *c.* 1905, showing the domestic-style architecture. *L. Hill Collection*

access from the down line being by trailing crossover.

Major J.W. Pringle made the Board of Trade inspection and issued the following report:*

RAILWAY DEPARTMENT

Board of Trade
8 Richmond Terrace
Whitehall
London S.W.

30 May 1908

Sir,

I have the honour to report for the information of the Board of Trade, that in compliance with the instructions contained in your Minute of the 21st inst., I made an inspection yesterday of the new works on the doubling between Exmouth Junction and Topsham Station on the L&SW Railway, authorised in the Session 1906 as Widening No. 2.

The works commence at the north end of Topsham Station, by an end-on junction with the down loop line, and terminate at Exmouth Junction; the total length being 4 miles 17.39 chains. The new line is on the east of the old single line and will be used for Down traffic.

The width of formation has been increased to 30 feet for both banks and cuttings, and the space between the old and new lines is 6 feet.

The existing fencing has been supplemented by a new length of 10 chains only of post and rails, 4 feet in height.

The width of the widest carriage to be used is 9 ft 3 ins, and the clearance at and over a height of 3 feet above rail level is 2 ft 4 ins.

The gradients and curves are similar to those on the old line. The steepest inclination is 1 in 82, and the sharpest curve has a radius of 24 chains (at Exmouth Junction).

The maximum earthwork in bank and cutting is 30 feet and 51 feet respectively, the soil throughout being sand with some slight traces of rock. I could detect no signs of failure in the new work in banks or cuttings.

The permanent way of the new line consists of second-hand steel single head rails, originally weighing 87 lbs per yd, and now stated to weigh 82 lbs per yard, in 30 feet lengths. The rails are laid in cast iron chairs weighing about 46 lbs each, and are secured thereto by oak keys. New creosoted sleepers, 12 to a rail length, of the usual dimensions (9 ft x 10 ins x 5 ins) are used, and the chairs are fastened to the sleepers by second-hand wrought iron spikes and new oak trenails. The fish plates and bolts are new, the former weigh 28½ lbs per pair. The line is ballasted with broken stone (Meldon) and the depth below the sleepers is stated to be 12 inches, and it is generally in a satisfactory condition.

Bridging - there are altogether eight bridges on the length. Two of these are overbridges, which were originally constructed for a double line and remain unaltered. Three are brick arched underbridges, and each with a single span of from 15 ft to 48 ft in length, which have been extended for the new line. The remainder are wrought iron underbridges with steel corrugated flooring and have been similarly extended. In each case there is a single span varying in length from 22 ft to 34 ft. I tested the iron and steel work in these underbridges under engine load and moderate deflections resulted. I understand that the engines which will be employed on the line are of the tank type with a total wheel-base of about 29½ feet, and a total weight in working order of 54 tons 2 cwts. [i.e. Adams' '415' class 4-4-2T. *Author*]. The bridges have sufficient theoretical strength for loads of this description.

There are no viaducts or tunnels on the length.

There are four private roads and one footway level crossings - the former are fitted

LONDON & SOUTH WESTERN R.

EXMOUTH

THE FLOWER OF LOVELY DEVON

MAGNIFICENT SCENERY

BEAUTIFUL HARBOUR

STEAMER EXCURSIONS

GOLF · TENNIS · CRICKET ·

EXPRESS TRAINS FROM WATERLOO IN 3¾ HOURS

WATERLOO STATION.   CHAS. J. OWENS, General Manager.

Eli Taylor, an Exmouth guard c. 1900.   *Dr T.F. Budden*   LSWR poster c. 1908.   *Author's Collection*

with the necessary gates.
Stations & Signalling -
Two new 'Halts' have been constructed as follows:
1.   Clyst St Mary & Digby at 2 miles 1 furlong
2.   Polsloe Bridge at 3 miles 7 furlongs 74 chains.
In each case there are two platforms, 120 feet in length, 6½ ft in width and 3 ft high. Adequate approaches have been provided to each platform from the adjoining public road, and the platforms are properly fenced and lighted, and provided with nameboards. There are no shelters on the platforms.
I recommend that these platforms be approved for use by steam motor carriages or ordinary trains of corresponding length.
The connections and signalling arrangements for double line working had not been completed at the time I made my inspection, and I was unable to examine them, or test the interlocking. It will be necessary when this work is completed to make a reinspection of the arrangements.
Subject therefore to this reinspection and to any requirement that may be made, I recommend the Board of Trade to provisionally sanction of [sic] these new works.
I have etc.
J.W. Pringle
Major

The branch was little affected by either of the World Wars apart from the opening on 23rd January, 1944 of Newcourt Sidings and the establishment of a Royal Marine Commando camp near Lympstone. After 1945 the development of road transport gradually made incursions into the traffic carried by the railway, though today the branch still carries a considerable amount of regular passenger traffic. In 1957, the number of tickets collected at Exmouth totalled 486,457, while Exeter Central's totalled 529,457; but the one and a half million journeys in 1959 had shrunk to half a million in 1963. In 1962 the cost of running the Exmouth line was £205,000, composed of: £141,000 movement costs, £14,000 terminal costs, £50,000 track and signalling. Fares only produced £110,000, leaving a loss of £95,000. Even so, when the Beeching Report was published on 27th March, 1963 it came as a great surprise that the line was threatened with closure. One thing which gave the line a great advantage over its critics was that all the stations, with the possible exception of Exton, were well-situated, thus destroying the sole advantage of the bus, in fact for buses, Lympstone is situated very inconveniently.

In the early 1960s about 225,000 tickets were issued at Exmouth station annually and over 400,000 collected, while in addition the station was used by about a thousand season ticket holders. In 1962 15,000 parcels were forwarded from Exmouth and 30,000 received on the passenger train service. Around 600 regular passengers used the first five trains every morning reaching Exeter before 9.00 am. Of this number, a proportion included college students and children for Exeter's main schools, whilst in the opposite direction commuters were accompanied by about 150 pupils for Exmouth's grammar and secondary schools. People preferred travelling to Exeter by train, the journey taking only 25 minutes, as against an average of about 50 minutes by bus. Polsloe Bridge Halt dealt with an average of about 600 passengers daily. Lympstone sold 200 tickets a day and in addition the station was used by 110 season ticket holders.

'M7' class 0-4-4T No. 30667 is seen north of Lympstone with an Exeter Central-Exmouth relief train, 15th June, 1958.   *S.C. Nash*

BR Standard class '3' 2-6-2T No. 82010 leaves Lympstone with the 11.20 am Exeter Central-Exmouth train, 31st May, 1959.   *S.C. Nash*

In 1957 the Southern Region announced that it intended changing over to diesel-electric traction and running a service of 20 minute frequency over the branch, but this scheme had not been put into practice by the time the Western Region took control on 1st January, 1963. The line was almost completely dieselised on 9th September, 1963 and to mark the occasion, British Railways, Western Region, held a luncheon at Exeter's Rougemont Hotel for the civic dignitaries of both Exeter Corporation and Exmouth Urban District Council, at which senior railway officials were present. The Exmouth UDC Railway Committee advertised the new service in the *Exmouth Journal* saying 'Use the service or lose your railway'.

As an essential preliminary to rendering the branch financially viable, a detailed survey was undertaken in order to reduce its operating costs. Significant details involved the singling of the line between Exmouth Junction and Topsham; unstaffing the three intermediate stations by introducing self-service ticket machines operated by passengers; the abolition of the locomotive shed and platform Nos. 3 and 4 at Exmouth (assuming the Budleigh Salterton branch services would be withdrawn). Apart from their detrimental effect on existing traffic it was impossible to implement all proposals by February 1965, but unstaffing arrangements were introduced on Sunday 28th February, 1965 and buildings at Polsloe Bridge, Exton and Lympstone were subsequently boarded up. Passengers purchased their tickets from guards equipped with an 'Omniprinter' ticket machine, the first of this type to be used in the West Country. Facilities for handing in and collecting parcels from Exton and Lympstone stations were withdrawn from the same date.

BR did not always use its available money wisely. Between January and March 1964 the concrete cable troughing laid from Exmouth Junction to Exmouth some 18 months previously, for intended improvements to the Southern Region's local railway telephone network, was taken up.

The Exmouth branch was the first line to be removed from the Beeching plan voluntarily - in other cases reprieve only came after the Minister's refusal to accept closure proposals. In April 1964 Ernest Marples, Minister of Transport, hinted that the Exeter to Exmouth service might escape the axe and this was confirmed on 20th August by the Plymouth Divisional Manager, Mr F.D. Pattisson, when he opened the 'New Railways' exhibition train at Exeter Central. Moves were afoot to reduce the operational costs of the branch to a minimum and it was originally intended to withdraw the Sunday service from 4th October, 1964 to 25th April, 1965, but this move was later rescinded.

The 15th March, 1967 saw the branch threatened again, as it was losing about £30,000 annually and was omitted from the map of lines scheduled for development. One interesting point made to keep the line open was that in the event of a national emergency, Exmouth was to receive 40,000 evacuees and a movement of such numbers could only be carried out by rail. A Consultation Meeting attended by management and staff was held on 20th June, but further meetings between local councils, the British Railways Board, the Minister of Transport and Members of Parliament, eventually resulted in the postponement of closure schemes.

With the closure of Exmouth signal box on 10th March, 1968, the four platform roads were reduced to one single line running into Platform No. 4. All signalling was removed, points spiked, clipped and padlocked pending later recovery. On 6th May, all facilities except Exmouth's booking office and hall were closed, conductor-guards covering intermediate traffic. By the autumn, additional savings were made by working all the branch services with just two 3-car units instead of three units previously and four in 1964. This reduced the timetable frequency and the capacity for strengthening peak services. Early in 1969, all surplus track was lifted from Exmouth station, its booking office and hall closed, leaving one entrance to a ticket kiosk erected on Platform No. 4 and the frontage of the station was leased as shops. It was about this time that revenue stopped declining and began to 'hold'.

The savings planned for 1968 enabled a convincing argument for the line's retention to be presented to the Minister of Transport, for on the political front, changes in legislation had taken place. In December 1967, the Western Region applied to the Transport Minister for a subsidy under Grant Aid procedure for which provision was made when the Transport bill was passed. This enabled uneconomic lines to qualify for a Ministry subsidy in cases where existing roads were inadequate to cater for alternative public transport. Both BR and local opinion believed this applied to the Exmouth branch.

Under the 1968 Transport Act, grants were on a one, two, or three yearly basis and revised annually. By the spring of 1969 the Exmouth branch was the only WR line to receive a three-year grant, conditional upon such economies as the elimination of surplus track and signalling. The Minister of Transport undertook to pay £85,000 in 1969, this amount being calculated on an assessment of net losses likely to be incurred over the period for which grant aid was being paid and covered all costs to which the Railway Board were liable in respect of the service, less receipts. Grants included provision for interest, administration and depreciation on a replacement cost basis, thus representing the full cost of retaining the service in the long term. The Minister had to be assured that every opportunity had been taken to produce a good service at the lowest possible cost, weighed against the social and economic benefits which it would bring. Economies were achieved with the previously described rationalisation schemes implemented during 1968, among them being the method of train signalling between Exmouth and Topsham. On closure of the former's signal box the electric tablet instrument at Topsham was recovered and the section worked on the 'one engine in steam' method, using a round, wooden train staff which permitted only one train at a time to travel from Topsham to Exmouth and back before the next train could be admitted. It had been intended that the double track from Exmouth Junction to Topsham would be singled as an economy measure during the period of the 1967-8 timetable, as is evidenced by the Working Timetable's route map for that period and the fact that the train service was based on crossing at Topsham or Exmouth Junction. During this period however, the railway engineering department's resources were being concentrated on singling the Salisbury to Exeter main line. This meant that it was neither financially nor physically possible to encompass this relatively small task, as regular maintenance of the remaining network still had to be undertaken. On the Exmouth branch, trains continued to use each track and from 5th May, 1969 the Working Timetable route map reverted to showing double line. This situation lasted until 1st May, 1972 when the map indicated the section as single line in anticipation of it actually occurring during the currency of the 1972-3 timetable, the engineering and signalling departments actually singling the line between Saturday 3rd February and Monday 5th February, 1973. The down line was lifted within the month, (work started on 15th February), except for a mile length which was retained while M5 motorway bridge work continued each side of Newcourt Sidings. The Department of the Environment contributed to the cost of these extensive underline bridges on the assurance that they would be carrying a single line.

In 1972 the grant was decreased from £85,000 to £82,000. In 1974 the annual cost of the line was:

	£
Train costs	75,000
Terminal costs	22,000
Track & signalling costs	51,000
Administration costs	19,000
	167,000

Receipts were only £71,000, the deficit of £96,000 being made up in the form of a grant from the Department of the Environment. In 1985 users of the branch comprised:

	percentage
Commuters	30
Shoppers	19
Scholars	15
Inter-City Connection	25
Friend/Relation visits	11

The planning of an urban relief road at Exmouth required the demolition of Exmouth station and so a new terminus was built, set back 80 yards from the existing one and planned to form part of a transport complex of car park, bus and railway station, its cost of £100,000 falling on Devon County Council. BR's preparatory work on the scheme began on 16th August, 1975 when the track serving the former Platform No. 4 was shortened by about 20 yards to allow a water main to be constructed. Ten days later, the 12.35 pm from St David's, comprised of cars W51190, 59421 and 51062, struck the buffers, pushing them back about 15 feet and de-railing the front car. By March 1976 the new station building was nearing completion. Track sections were laid and ballasted into the new platform, formerly No. 2. On Sunday 2nd May, the existing single line was slewed into the new platform line. The first train into the station was the 1.56 pm from St David's. The following day a completely new Lympstone Commando station was opened between Lympstone and Exton, specially to serve about 1,400 men in barracks at the Royal Marines Commando Training Centre. British Rail provided champagne to celebrate the opening of its Lympstone Commando station, and the inaugural train, the 10.24 am from St David's, carried a special headboard bearing the British Rail emblem and the

An up dmu pauses at Exton station, 6th June, 1970.   *John R. Bonser*

Lympstone: Set P576 comprising class '119' Nos. W51062/59421/51090 arriving at Lympstone on 22nd April, 1976 with the 2.45 pm Exeter Central-Exmouth.   *Author*

Royal Marines' insignia. However, there was no official welcoming committee for the inaugural train at Devon County Council's new Exmouth station. The Commando station increased the traffic to the branch, which was already one and a half million passengers a year in 1975. In December 1976, Topsham, Exton and Lympstone stations were improved at a cost of £15,000 shared equally by BR and Devon County Council. The work involved replacing some of the old buildings with modern passenger shelters and installing new lighting. The completed bus and rail interchange opened on 3rd June, 1980, but three years later it diminished in importance as local bus services, except for the summer season Sandy Bay service, were re-routed to exclude the town's bus station.

In 1995 a second new station, Digby & Sowton, opened, as detailed in Chapter Four.

From 13th October, 1996 operation of the train service has passed to South Wales & West Railway. Together with Railtrack Great Western, the new owner of the infrastructure, these companies replace the former British Rail administration.

The exterior of Exmouth's bus and rail stations, 18th July, 1989. The new station came into use on 2nd May, 1976 and the official opening of the completed interchange took place on 3rd June, 1980.   *Author*

Exeter Queen Street looking 'down' *c.* 1921. An 0-4-4T on the left is leaving for Exmouth. The goods yard is on the right with tree trunks laden on wagons nearest the camera. Notice the complex track arrangement and partly-assembled pointwork in the foreground. *Lens of Sutton*

Exeter Central: Queen Street frontage including crescent of shops, photographed in 1978.

Author

Chapter Four

Description of the Line:
Exeter-Topsham

Until the extension of most services to St David's in 1976, the majority of trains for Exmouth started from Exeter's Central station, (171 m. 30 ch.). Opened on 19th July, 1860, it completed the line from Salisbury. Formerly known as Queen Street, the original station consisted of two platforms served by loops from the through lines, the whole shrouded by an all-over roof. To cope with Exmouth trains, a bay platform was first added at the east end of the down platform, followed by another at the east end of the up platform. In 1925 a scissors crossing was laid between the up through and the platform lines and the up platform lengthened to 1,207 feet in order that two up trains could be handled simultaneously. On 15th June, 1927 a new 'A' signal box at the east end of the layout replaced former 'A' and 'B' boxes, the former 'C' at the west end being renamed 'B'. Accommodation was still inadequate and it was obvious that the station would have to be rebuilt. In March 1931 a two-storey structure was planned, estimated to cost £50,000-£60,000, but was whittled down to a more economic £35,000 single storey building, the SR being afraid that it would not be able to sublet a larger building. A planned New North Road entrance was abandoned, the sole way in to be from Queen Street. The City Council inspected the plans and was very unhappy to see that plans for the new station were similar to that which had recently been built at Exmouth, believing that the city should have something better.

After some re-thinking, the Directors decided in May 1931 to erect a three-storey building in red brick and reinforced concrete with trains in the basement and a two-storey crescent above, 259 feet in length.

Work started in September 1931. The old roof and timber buildings were demolished and replaced by modern brick structures including pleasant buffets on both platforms. (These were closed on 5th September, 1971.) On the down side, a spacious concourse was built with shops fronting Queen Street, which crossed the line at the station's west end. The offices included a bombproof control room with oversight of all SR territory west of Salisbury. Both platforms were widened and re-roofed and the down platform lengthened to 950 feet. A new entrance embodying a passimeter booking office was constructed on New North Road which bridges the station at its eastern end. This entrance was closed during World War II and closed completely about 1966 but was reopened on 2nd July, 1984. The rebuilt station was completed and re-named on 1st July, 1933. The eastern end of the station was controlled by Exeter Central 'A' box with 90 levers operated by one signalman and a booking boy; the western box, Exeter Central 'B' at the head of the incline of 1 in 37 down to St David's, had 35 levers and was operated by one man. In 1951 the station had a weekday average of 120 trains stopping or passing through and issued a daily average of 800 tickets, including seasons.

Seventy-three coaches could be stabled in the carriage sidings, while on the up side a brick goods shed and 10-road yard was provided.

Following the removal of redundant sidings during the late 1960s, cement trains

Exeter Central looking west. Bulleid 'Pacific' No. 34104 *Bere Alston* heads the up 'Atlantic Coast Express', 2nd September, 1959.   *H.B. Priestley*

Exeter Central: the 11.52 am Exmouth-Exmouth Central terminates at the bay platform on 7th August, 1984.   *Author*

from Westbury provided the sole remaining freight traffic, until this, too, ceased around 20 years later. The lifting of the facing crossover at the east end of the station in November 1973 effectively confined all down arrivals to the down side and rendered the up bay (platform No. 4) suitable only for departures. A train indicator was provided at the Queen Street and New North Road entrances facing incoming passengers directly after they left the ticket barrier and showed the platform number of the next departure for Exmouth. Branch trains which terminated at Central, either in the down bay (platform No. 1) or down main, could be signalled to return to Exmouth from these lines, as in steam days, when they normally used the up or down bay platforms. The choice was determined by whether the train was making a connection with an up or down main line train, or whether the locomotive was diagrammed to run round the train, since only the up bay had a run-round loop. When a train ran into the down bay, the use of the station pilot or a turnover engine was required to release the train engine.

In 1984 when Central closed at 8.30 pm on 26th October until 6 am on 29th October to allow work on Phase 1 of the Exeter Multiple Aspect Signalling (MAS) scheme to be completed, the service from Exmouth worked by 3-car dmu Nos. W51311, 59480 and 51326 terminated at Polsloe Bridge. The resignalling extended as far as Exmouth Junction box as part of the major modernisation of signalling based on Exeter St David's power box. Colour light signals at the Central station were controlled from the Central signal box (former 'A', 'B' had closed on 23rd February, 1970) until its closure on 6th May, 1985. From this date signals were linked with the power box at St David's resulting in the down line becoming reversible, the up remaining unidirectional. If a train leaves St David's for Central via the down (reversible) line, and from St David's platform 3 it can only proceed via the down line, it has to keep to the down side at Central as the first facing crossover is east of Central station. As a train to the Exmouth line is 'approach controlled' at Exmouth Junction (i.e. the junction signal is held at red until a train is a certain distance from it), the previous signal can show only a yellow aspect when cleared for an Exmouth train. As this previous signal is the departure signal at Central, it means that an Exmouth train only ever leaves under a yellow aspect irrespective of whether it starts from platforms 1, 2 or 3.

From Exeter Central the main line rises on a gradient of 1 in 100 to Lion's Holt Halt (170 miles 72 chains). On 7th October, 1946 it was re-named St James' Park Halt after the nearby Exeter City Football Club ground. The up platform, which previously had a small waiting shelter, is only 119 feet in length compared with 244 feet of the down platform, the latter being extended in May 1928. As the up platform is mostly used for picking up passengers it does not need to be so long as passengers can step into the coaches which draw up alongside regardless of the train's length. The station is sited in a cutting and this situation, combined with the gradient, sometimes led to starting problems for up trains. Beyond the halt the line enters the 262 yds-long brick-lined Black Boy tunnel, scene of a mishap on 25th November, 1865 when a down train ran into a roof fall and the passengers had only just started out on foot when a second fall crushed a carriage. Twenty-three feet of roof had fallen due to workmen failing to pack the space over the arch and so leaving room for rock to drop onto the bricks. One line was re-opened on 3rd December and the other the following day.

Class '150' No. 150 239 is seen at St James' Park Halt with a train from Exmouth on 17th October, 1992.   *Roger Palmer*

Mount Pleasant Road Halt in the foreground and Exmouth Junction reception sidings with the concrete works beyond, seen in 1927.   *Courtesy 'Railway Engineer'*

Mount Pleasant Road Halt, (170 m. 38 ch.) at the eastern portal of the tunnel, was closed on 2nd January, 1928.

To the north of the line was Exmouth Junction marshalling yard which in 1952 handled 700 wagons daily in 10 parallel roads, with 30 departures and 27 arrivals. On the up side was also the Southern Railway's concrete works established in 1913 by the LSWR chief engineer J.W. Jacomb-Hood. Among items made there were mileage, gradient and fencing posts, electric light standards, platform coping slabs, and sections for the construction of buildings and footbridges. The works closed in 1963 under rationalisation as Taunton had been set up as a pre-stressed concrete depot and therefore the Exeter depot was superfluous. Steel principals and stanchions for the concrete sheds at Exmouth Junction came from Queen Street station when it was demolished.

From 4th December, 1967 the site has been used for the Exeter Coal Distribution Depot, but this is no longer served by rail. The adjacent carriage and wagon works is now a Railtrack depot. Nearby was the Exmouth Junction motive power depot opened in 1880 and modernised in 1927 and 1928, a new running shed being built (270 ft by 249 ft) with 13 roads under cover. Over a hundred engines were once shedded at this SR Western District motive power headquarters which embraced all SR territory west of Salisbury. Its coaling plant could deal with two engines simultaneously and the 65 ft turntable, originally electrically operated, was later vacuum-worked. The shed closed on 6th March, 1967.

Leaving the main line which continues eastwards, the branch curves right at Exmouth Junction (170 m. 27 ch.), a speed limit of 25 mph being imposed for branch trains at this spot. In the fork at the actual junction, stood the twice-enlarged LSWR signal box. When the line was doubled to Topsham it was given a new 33-lever frame of which one lever was spare. Latterly it contained a 49-lever Stevens-type locking frame controlling main and branch line trains and also the entrance to the locomotive depot, the pre-cast concrete depot and the sidings on each side of the line. Train signalling between the box and Topsham was controlled by Sykes' lock-and-block. When the LSWR box became life-expired, a replacement was built a few yards to the west and opened 17th November, 1959. Its siting and equipment made provision for future access to the proposed diesel-electric multiple-unit carriage sheds, which in the event were never built. The basic structure of the new cabin was load-carrying brickwork with reinforced concrete floors on steel frame supports. It contained a 64-lever Westinghouse-style 'A3' lever frame with catch handle locking actuation and 'L' type lever locks and circuit controllers. Branch signalling, then by three-position block using standard BR (SR) instruments, was superseded from 5th February, 1973 by the Tokenless Block System, worked by acceptance lever with continuous track circuiting.

From 16th January, 1988 Exmouth Junction signal box was re-fitted to align with the MAS scheme and take over the duties of Topsham and Pinhoe (on the Salisbury line) boxes, Topsham closing on 30th January and Pinhoe on 14th February. The double track junction was replaced by a ladder with a single turnout. From 14th February, 1988, the date the installation was complete, Exmouth Junction was coded 'EJ'. Instead of a signalling panel which would hitherto have been fitted, visual display units (VDU) were installed. The

Bulleid 'Pacific' No. 35023 *Holland-Afrika Line* passes Exmouth Junction signal box as it heads the down 'Devon Belle' *c.* 1952. The Exmouth Branch sweeps away to the right. Note the the coaling stage at Exmouth Junction shed in the distance. The signal box was closed and its replacement, shown on page 38, opened on 15th November 1959.

M. Daly

Exmouth Junction, showing the reception sidings, concrete works and engine shed. Polsloe Bridge Halt can be seen centre right. The site of Mount Pleasant Halt is on the extreme left, near the eastern portal of Black Boy tunnel, the station was closed in 1928.

Reproduced from the 25", 1932 Ordnance Survey Map

BR Standard class '3MT' 2-6-2T No. 82017 passing Exmouth Junction with the 11.40 am
Exmouth-Exeter Central in October 1953.   *T. Reardon*

Exmouth Junction signal box with the Exmouth branch curving away to the right, 7th August,
1984. Notice the WR-pattern signal and disconnected track on the left.   *Author*

hardware used a tracker ball, cursor and keyboard inputting commands to a computer. It was the first installation of its kind on BR. Called SDS (Signalman's Display System) it is fully compatible with solid state interlocking and an integrated electronics control centre, unlike the other VDU system then at Leicester. VDUs show the track layout and level crossings at Topsham and Pinhoe which are monitored by the Exmouth Junction signalman using closed circuit television. Signal functions and train movements were simulated to make testing as authentic as possible. A second VDU displays other information such as alarms and is used to set up a train description before transfer to the track layout monitor. The two VDUs are interchangeable.

Beyond the junction the line runs straight for 1¼ miles. At 0 miles 12 chains on the west side of the line was a siding serving the Exeter Brick & Tile Company, later the Western Counties Brick Company, at its north end, and the Domestic Chemical Company (previously 'Collard's') at its south end. Total length of the brick siding was 6.7 chains, of which 3.3 chains were privately-owned. The length of the chemical siding was 3.3 chains. Access from the branch was by a trailing crossover off the up line operated by Exmouth Junction signal box, which also controlled a trailing crossover added between the up and down branch lines immediately south of the siding, to enable freight trains from Exmouth Junction to regain the correct track when proceeding to Exmouth. Traffic to and from the siding circulated via Exmouth Junction marshalling yard, and comprised outgoing bricks from adjacent clay pits and ingoing chemicals for re-packaging and subsequent distribution by road. This siding was the responsibility of the Topsham station master, although Polsloe Bridge Halt was in the jurisdiction of Exeter Central.

Unusual movements were necessary to service the siding and the 1934 instructions stated that traffic for the sidings must be propelled with a brake van leading, from the up reception road, or the up main line at Exmouth Junction, through the crossover leading to the down main line and brought to a stand when the engine had passed clear of the up Exmouth branch trailing points. The train was then permitted to be drawn along the up Exmouth branch as far as the points leading to the siding, where it had to be brought to a stand. The van brakes were then applied by the shunter, after which the ingoing wagons were uncoupled and drawn into the Topsham end of the siding. Outgoing wagons were gravitated to the Topsham end prior to the engine drawing into this end with the ingoing wagons.

All the vehicles were then moved along the siding in the direction of Exmouth Junction to a point inside the gate where the ingoing wagons were required to be detached. The shunter then released the brakes of the van standing on the up Exmouth line and allowed it to gravitate towards the stop blocks at the Topsham end of the siding, after which the engine and outgoing wagons were backed on to the van and coupled to it. If it was impracticable for the van to be placed in the siding, it was gravitated, with the shunter in charge of the brake, along the up line in the direction of Topsham to a point clear of the siding connection and after the van brake had been fully applied and the brake wheel secured, the locomotive and wagons drawn from the siding and coupled to the van. On the return journey to Exmouth Junction marshalling sidings, the train had to be brought to

Polsloe Bridge Halt, view looking 'up'. The passengers seem to be camera-shy and have turned their backs to the photographer. The Exmouth Junction coal hopper can be seen on the top right-hand corner.   *Lens of Sutton*

Polsloe Bridge Halt on 16th August, 1978 after singling of track which had taken place by February 1973.   *Author*

a stand on the down main line clear of the up Exmouth branch trailing points and propelled through the crossover road to the up reception siding, or up main line. The brick siding was taken out of use on 12th May, 1967 and the chemical siding on 7th January, 1973. Beyond the site of these sidings, from 1973-1988, the double line became single (there was a speed restriction of 25 mph through the points), the former down line being lifted as an economy measure. (After 1988, as previously mentioned, the single line commenced at Exmouth Junction points.) The line falls at 1 in 100 to Polsloe Bridge Halt (0 m. 34 ch.), situated on the embankment immediately after crossing the main Taunton to West of England road. The original platforms built of timber at a cost of £243 only accommodated three coaches, but were replaced by a longer concrete construction in 1928, the parts being cast in the nearby depot. The *Railway Engineer* of that year recorded:

> . . . the reinforced concrete slabbing forming the surface of the platforms rests on direct concrete brackets, which are particularly light and simple in design, and by extending the back legs of these brackets up above platform level they have been made to serve in addition as the posts for the fencing along the back of the platforms.
>
> The railway at the halt is on an embankment, and the design in question was adopted on that account. Access to the platforms from the public road below is gained by concrete staircases; there is a small combined shelter and booking office, also in concrete with asbestos roofing, on the down platform, and a concrete name board with white concrete letters on a black background [Actually these colours were reversed. *Author*] is provided on each platform.

The now trackless down platform is 488 ft in length and the up, the only one in use following singling, 607 feet long. Later modifications gave the up platform a waiting shelter at the Exeter end while a second shelter was centrally sited on the down platform only. As the original ticket office served the down platform and was some distance from the path leading up to the other platform, the ticket clerk came across with a ticket rack just before a train was due. At some later date the ticket office was closed and a ticket booth incorporated in the down platform shelter, to which a small porch was added. The original ticket office was still opened at busy periods and at weekends to supplement the office on the platform. During morning rush hours it was usual for workers to pack the up platform, while on other occasions the down platform might be crowded with day-trippers.

The line continues to fall at 1 in 100, becomes level and then rises at 1 in 100, decreasing to 1 in 400 to the summit at 1 m. 50 ch. The line then descends for 3¼ miles to beyond Topsham. A half-mile descent at 1 in 120 ends at Clyst St Mary & Digby Halt (2 m. 12 ch.). Closed from 29th September, 1948 and its sleeper-built structure dismantled soon after, it was situated on the north side of the bridge over the Exeter to Sidmouth road. In addition to being of use to the village one mile distant, it served Digby's Mental Hospital.

Sowton Industrial Estate has developed nearby and the first sod of Digby & Sowton station (2 m. 20 ch.) was turned on 9th November, 1994. Funded by Devon County Council and Tesco Stores Ltd, it opened on 23rd May, 1995. The platform is on the site of the former down line and consists of concrete beams

Digby & Sowton station looking north, seen on a very wet day in February 1997.
Geoff Newhouse

Connecting minibus to St David's station leaves the road level entrance to Digby & Sowton station, 11th March, 1997. *Author*

covered with paving bricks, the whole supported on breeze block pillars. The station is quite basic with a metal bench seat in a small shelter. Another shelter is provided at road level for passengers using a minibus service. An adjacent car park has 330 spaces, but the number of cars there is usually in single figures as, apart from those proceeding to and from the Sowton Industrial Estate, the station is little used at present. A footpath links the station with the Estate.

The line falls at 1 in 250 to Digby's siding (2 m. 48 ch.) which trailed off the up line, the ground frame being opened by Sykes' lock and plunger from Topsham box, inwards traffic being operated via that station. A line was run across the hospital grounds to a point near the Ballroom, for the purpose of taking building materials from the brickyard at Exmouth to the site of the new hospital. This siding was inspected by Colonel Rich of the Board of Trade on 2nd May, 1884. Four years later when the building was finished the track was lifted except for a length of 5.1 chains used by coal wagons shunted in every fortnight or so, three or four at a time, bringing steam coal for the boilers and domestic coal for the hospital fires. When the line was single the siding was controlled by tablet, but on doubling was worked from a 3-lever ground frame, two of these levers being spare. The frame was controlled by Sykes' apparatus, permission having to be sought from Topsham signal box before the frame could be opened. When permission was granted, Topsham up starting signal was locked until the ground frame was closed. The siding closed on being relinquished by the hospital on 10th January, 1957.

The line steepens to 1 in 100 falling for a mile, crossing the motorway access road by a two-span concrete bridge erected 1973-74; not far down the gradient were Newcourt Sidings (2 m. 71 ch.). These American Naval Depot sidings were built with remarkable speed. At 12.10 pm on Saturday 2nd October, 1943 the United States Navy authorities asked the SR Western Divisional superintendent to meet them at 2.30 pm that afternoon to discuss making a temporary siding on a green field so that 150 wagons of stores on their way from the North might be unloaded. The Divisional engineer also attended the meeting and arranged to have sufficient material to lay 1,200 ft of siding delivered by 11 am on Monday the 4th. He was almost as good as his word for it was there by noon. Twenty-four hours later the Americans had laid 1,000 ft of track, the SR Divisional engineer's staff had laid the connection and raised a shallow embankment to link with the siding. By noon on Wednesday wagons were in position and by 5 pm the siding was complete with signalling.* The ground frame was replaced by a signal box on 23rd January, 1944, which also controlled a crossover. Eventually the depot had three sidings with lengths of 28.5, 27.3 and 26.7 chains.

In more recent years they were used by the Ministry of Defence as a Naval Stores Depot. The double gates were an unusual feature; they protected a public footpath which crossed the connection leading to the sidings. These sidings were generally worked by a timetabled trip from Exmouth Junction, rather than by the daily branch freight. The platelayer's-hut-style concrete signal box was worked by a porter-signalman responsible to the Topsham station master. When he was not in the box, he dealt with consignment notes and other paperwork and also maintained the signal lamps. The box was converted to a ground frame on 5th February, 1973 when the line was singled.

* Darwin B., *War on the Line*.

Newcourt sidings ground frame on 24th October, 1978. This prefabricated building was used as a signal box from 23rd January, 1944 to 3rd February, 1973 when it became a ground frame. Its eventual closure came in 1986. *Author*

No. 142 024 passes the former Newcourt ground frame. The ground frame hut is just visible between the far end of the unit and a tree. The picture was taken on 7th October, 1986 following the removal of the siding leading to the MOD depot. *Stephen Cummins*

Since this date, a train wishing to work the sidings was required to stop just clear of the points with the head or tail of the train standing on the short track circuit adjacent to the facing end of the points. When the circuit had been occupied for a minute, a released indication was given for the ground frame interlocking lever which was then operable. If a train was shut in, before it could leave the signalman had to be contacted and if in a position to do so, he gave a release for the interlocking lever. The guard was responsible for making sure that no vehicle was left foul of the single line and was required to advise the signalman when the ground frame was returned to normal.

In the 1970s Exeter Riverside Yard to Newcourt trips were usually worked by a locomotive of class '25', '31', '33'', or more rarely a '47'. During the 1983 Falklands War the sidings experienced a greater than normal frequency of movements, but following the crisis saw little traffic. Sometimes when vans were taken down they had to be returned as no one could be found to open the gates into the MOD property.*

The last train out of the siding was at 9.52 am on 26th March, 1986 loaded with 70 tons of rail and 100 tons of chaired sleepers bound for Trackwork Ltd, Doncaster. The sidings had been closed to normal traffic about a month earlier.

A steel girder bridge, with a central pier crossing over the M5 motorway was installed on 30th March, 1975. About 10 months earlier a temporary bridge was built to the east of the site, track laid across and the old line slewed to connect. A permanent bridge was then built on the site of the line, track laid, a reconnection made and the temporary bridge removed; this procedure also applied to the access road bridge mentioned above.

Topsham (4 m. 26 ch.), the most important intermediate station on the branch, still has its double track retained as a passing loop. The former 10 mph speed restriction has now been raised to 25 mph. Up trains have a straight run, but the down loop is curved at both ends, the turnout at the north end having previously been part of a crossover. Topsham, like Lympstone and Exmouth, was an Electric Tablet block post comprising 23 levers with returnable tablet. The signal box, from 20th May, 1973, operated lifting barriers instead of swinging level crossing gates over the main Exeter to Exmouth road until 1988, when the barriers became remotely controlled from Exmouth Junction. The redundant box then became a Grade II listed building available for business use. The down platform is 475 ft in length and the up 508 ft long, both having concrete extensions at their southern ends. The original platforms were rather low and portable wooden steps had to be used to assist invalids.

The red brick station building on the up platform, designed by Sir William Tite, received a cream rendering in Southern Railway days. The station building and station master's house are now offices, the date 1860 still visible on their exterior. The substantial flat awning, now removed, over the centre of the up platform was supported on five columns. Flower baskets hung from the awning as they did on most of the branch line's stations. The station was closed to goods traffic on 4th December, 1967, but the brick-built goods shed was used for light industry and a builders' merchant until its demolition in 1993, the site being sold for housing. Principal traffic for its six sidings included timber and domestic coal. Topsham dispatched by passenger train, raspberries, cherries

* Information from Eric Youldon.

Topsham station, *c.* 1905 view looking 'up'. *Lens of Sutton*

Topsham station, *c.* 1910: a '415' class 4-4-2T heads an up train. *Lens of Sutton*

Topiary at Topsham: up end of down platform, 24th October, 1978.   *Author*

Topsham station up platform, 18th July, 1989.   *Author*

Topsham: the former goods shed, now used by a builders' merchant, 18th July, 1989.   *Author*

and plums, practically every train in the season carrying fruit. Locally caught salmon were also sent from the station. One local nursery specialised in orchids and 20 to 30 consignments were sent off daily. The station had a lilac hedge and, in spring, the staff returned one evening, cut the blooms and dispatched them to Covent Garden, the proceeds going to the LSWR or SR Orphanage. Topsham station was lit by gas until 1976, the gas pipes having been renewed in 1958. The redundant piping was used unofficially to strengthen the straight letters of 'Topsham', done in topiary and a feature of the station since 1947; the curved letters were supported by signalling and telegraph wire.

In the 1920s Topsham was staffed by a station master, two clerks, two signalmen, a porter-signalman, a goods checker, a leading porter and a porter. Porters were required to do shunting, there being no official shunter. The station was partially unstaffed from 28th February, 1965 and fully unstaffed from 6th May, 1968. The box had a roster of three signalmen whose duties also included sweeping the station and also those at Exton, Lympstone Commando and Lympstone. Topsham was the first station (as opposed to halt) on the branch and its name gave rise to a rather naive schoolboy riddle: Why can't they run a non-stop train from Exeter to Exmouth? Answer: Because the first station stops 'em.

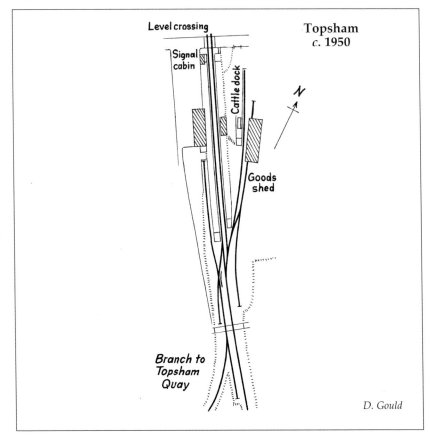

D. Gould

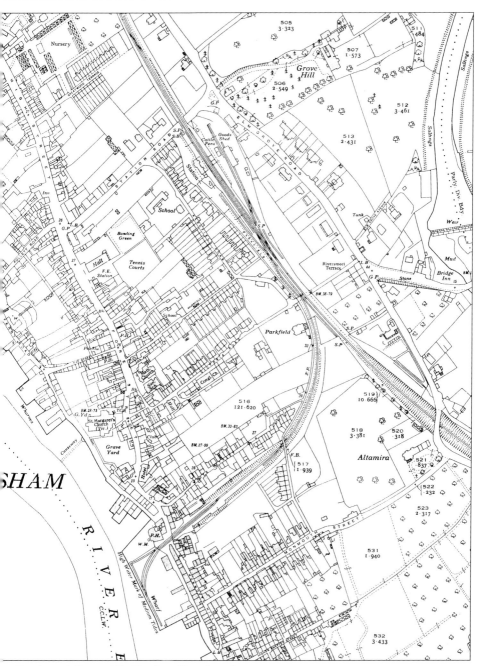

Topsham station and the Topsham Quay branch.
Reproduced from the 25″, 1936 Ordnance Survey Map

TOPSHAM.

Dock siding.—Bogie coaches must not be shunted alongside the dock.

Quay line.—This line, the length of which is 32 chains, connects with the up sidings at Topsham station by means of hand points, which must be kept normally set for the up siding and padlocked when not in use, the key being kept in the signal box at Topsham.

The gradients of the line, falling in the direction of the quay, are as follows : 1 in 300 for a distance of 1 chain ; 1 in 38 for a distance of 4¾ chains ; 1 in 44 for a distance of 11 chains ; 1 in 150 for a distance of 4½ chains, the remainder of the line being level.

Catch points are provided in the Quay line at a spot about 10½ chains from the points in the up sidings at Topsham and are operated by a hand lever, which is secured to lie normally for the catch. These catch points are facing for trains proceeding in the direction of the quay.

Sprags must be kept on the Quay line at intervals of every 50 yards for use in case of emergency.

The Quay line is worked as a siding, only one engine in steam being allowed on the line at one time. All movements to and from the quay must be carried out during daylight and must be under the control of a competent member of the Topsham station staff, who will be primarily responsible for all movements over the Quay line.

At the foot of the incline the line crosses the public road on the level before entering on the quay. Double gates are provided on either side of the road at this crossing, which must be kept normally closed across the railway and padlocked.

As the gates do not fence the road when open for the passage of railway vehicles, portable trestles and chains are provided for placing across the public road when such vehicles require to pass over the crossing, and these trestles and chains, when not in use, are secured to posts and padlocked, the key being kept in the signal box at Topsham.

The following instructions must be carefully observed in connection with the working of goods and ballast trains to and from the quay :—

The only engines permitted to run over the Quay line are Nos. 177-179 inc., 181-183 inc., 185, 187, 189, 191-201 inc., 203, 204, 207, 212-214 inc., 216-218 inc., 221-225 inc., and 227-236 inc.

The loads of goods and ballast trains on the Quay line must not exceed the equivalent of 8 loaded goods wagons and a brake van.

A train proceeding to the quay must be propelled from Topsham station and drawn on the return journey. The special brake van which has been provided for use on the Quay line must at all times be attached at the leading end on the forward journey and at the rear on the return journey. Two men must ride in this brake van, the senior of whom will be responsible for the proper manipulation of the hand brake. A good supply of sprags must be kept in this brake van for use in case of emergency.

Before reaching the catch points on the incline, the train must be brought to a stand to enable the second man travelling with the train to alight and hold the catch points in the correct position for the safe passage of the train.

On reaching the points leading to the sidings on the quay, situated on the station side of the level crossing gates, the train must again be brought to a stand, and, after the man in charge has satisfied himself that it has been made secure by the application of the van brake and hand brakes and sprags, he and his assistant must place the trestles and chains in position across the road and exhibit red flags on either side of the barrier. Shunting operations to the quay sidings will then be commenced. The second man with the train must remain at the crossing with a red flag in his hand to control road vehicles that may approach the crossing.

In consequence of the very sharp curves leading to the quay sidings, the engine must not in any circumstances, be permitted to proceed beyond the public road in the direction of the quay.

When the shunting at the quay has been completed, the wagons to be taken to the station must be marshalled with the brake van at the rear and well clear of the gates on the station side of the level crossing. The van brake must be applied and secured by the man in charge of the train, who must then assist the second man to withdraw the chains and trestles, place them in their proper position, secure them by padlock, and close and lock the gates in their normal position across the railway on either side of the public road. The men must then rejoin the van, and, after the man in charge has released the brake, the train must, after the exchange of the necessary bell signals with the Signalman at Topsham station in accordance with the prescribed code, proceed to the station.

After passing over the catch points on the incline, the man in charge must be careful to satisfy himself that these points have fallen into their correct position.

A Driver proceeding from the quay to the station must give one long whistle on approaching the top of the incline to warn people passing over the public foot crossing at Topsham station.

Extract from 1934 Working Timetable, giving working procedure for the Topsham Quay line.

Chapter Five

The Topsham Quay Branch

At the southern end of the station a branch 32 chains in length led down to the quay. The formation of this line is now a road called 'Holman Way'; the footbridge spanning it formerly crossed the railway. When the E&E was under construction, some of the earth excavated from the cuttings was used to construct a new wharf, the Town Quay being extended 80 feet into the estuary and connected with the Steamer Quay, purchased by the LSWR, the intermediate space containing three small quays being filled in. The LSWR made this considerable outlay at Topsham because of the difficulty of establishing docks at Exmouth. The quay line was opened to traffic on 23rd September, 1861. A notice from the LSWR traffic manager's office said that the water alongside the quay had been deepened and ships lying alongside the quay could discharge cargoes of coal, timber, stone, slates and other merchandise direct into rail trucks which could then be conveyed to Queen Street station where ample accommodation was provided for storing coal and other traffic. The freight charge from the quay to Exeter was 1s. 6d. a ton for a minimum consignment of four tons, loaded and unloaded at owner's expense.

The Quay line connected with the up sidings at Topsham station by means of hand points which were required to be kept normally set for the up siding and padlocked when not in use, the key being kept in the signal box. The gradients of the line, falling in the direction of the Quay, were as follows: 1 in 300 for 1 chain; 1 in 38 for a distance of 4¾ chains; 1 in 44 for 11 chains; 1 in 150 for a distance of 4½ chains, the remainder of the line being level. Catch points were provided about 10½ chains from the points in the up siding and were operated by a hand lever, secured to lie normally for the catch. These points faced trains proceeding in the direction of the Quay. As an additional safety measure, sprags were kept at intervals of 50 yards for use in case of emergency.

The Quay line was worked as a siding, only one engine in steam being allowed on it at one time. All movements to and from the Quay were required to be carried out during daylight. At the foot of the incline, the line crossed a public road on the level before entering the quay. Double gates were provided on either side of the road and were normally closed across the railway and padlocked. As the gates did not fence the road when open for the passage of railway vehicles, portable trestles and chains were provided for placing across the public road and when not in use, were secured to posts and padlocked, the key being kept in the signal box at Topsham.

Trains were restricted to the equivalent of eight loaded goods wagons, but in wet weather, four was the usual limit. Perhaps introduced after the 1925 runaway (*see below*), a special light brake van was always required to be at the Quay end of the train. It had a short van body containing a seat for two men, while single plank sides around the open platform prevented the large supply of sprags from being vibrated off. The clasp brakes were operated by a handwheel located centrally on the transverse axis, but longitudinally slightly

Two aerial views of the Topsham Quay branch from picture postacards. *Above*: view looking north with Topsham station at centre right. *Below:* a pre-1925 view. The quay line can be seen curving round from near the top left through the centre of the picture. *(Both) Topsham Museum*

The Topsham Quay branch tracks crossing the road next to the 'Steam Packet Inn' at the foot of Monmouth Hill. *Topsham Museum*

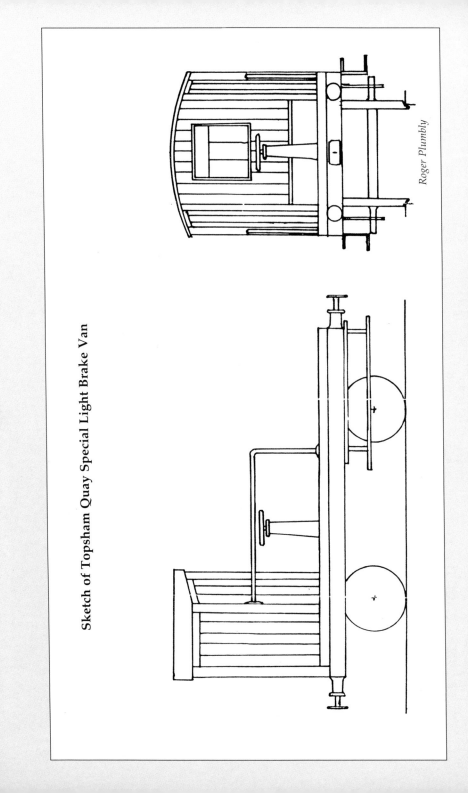

Sketch of Topsham Quay Special Light Brake Van

Roger Plumbly

nearer the shelter end. Two men rode on the van, the senior of whom was responsible for working the handbrake. A good supply of sprags was kept in the brake van for use in case of emergency. Before reaching the catch points on the incline, the train had to be brought to a stand to enable the second man travelling with the train to alight and hold the catch points in the correct position for the safe passage of the train. Before this special brake van was used, two porters were required to walk beside the trucks ready to thrust in sprags should this prove necessary. Even when the brake van was used, the Topsham porter threw grit from the ballast on the rails to give the wheels more grip. In 1925 five trucks ran away down the gradient. As it happened, part of the quay had previously slipped and the wagons derailed into the pit made by the subsidence. The wagons were hauled back by a steam crane.

When new in 1892, 'B4' class 0-4-0Ts Nos. 88, 91/2 were shedded at Exmouth Junction for working the siding. The 'O2' class 0-4-4 tank engines were the largest locomotives permitted to work the line and in consequence of the very sharp curves leading to the Quay sidings, a locomotive was not in any circumstances allowed to proceed beyond the public road in the direction of the Quay. On returning, an engine driver was required to give one long whistle when near the top of the incline to warn people passing over the public foot crossing south of the station.

One of the important commodities unloaded at Topsham was guano which was lifted out of ships' holds in baskets. An engine went down to the Quay in the morning to collect wagons which were then worked from Topsham goods yard to Odam's siding by the afternoon goods. Barrels came by rail to the quay from Peterhead for sprats to be packed in and were then loaded into the Tuborg lager boats to form a cargo for their return journey. Bundles of half-pound boxes of smoked sprats were sent off by rail from the quay. Latterly the Quay branch was worked three times a week until its closure in 1957, rails and sleepers being lifted in August the following year.

The footbridge over the branch remains *in situ* and is seen here in 1996. As can be seen a road (Holman Way) now uses part of the course of the railway line.   *Ron White*

Recently laid track awaiting alignment on the rebuilt River Clyst viaduct, photographed 6th December, 1960.   *S.P. Derek*

'700' class 0-6-0 No. 30691 propelling wagons laden with girders of the old Clyst viaduct, 14th May, 1961. A mess coach and wagon are on the former alignment.   *S.P. Derek*

Chapter Six

Description of Line:
Topsham-Exmouth

Beyond Topsham the single line reaches the coast and follows the shore for the rest of the route to Exmouth. The line crosses the 114 yds-long five-span River Clyst Viaduct, the pillars of which were built to allow for a second line should this have become necessary. In 1959 the spans required replacement. A temporary siding was laid for the contractors on the seaward side of the embankment south of the viaduct. It was fortunate that the piers were built for double line, because during the summer the hitherto unused part of them was cut away to take the new girders at a lower level. This enabled the decking strips on which the track bed was laid to be supported on the girders themselves, rather than between, as was the case with the old bridge. On the Sundays in October the new spans were lowered into position after which the decking was surfaced with concrete. During the autumn of 1960 ballast was laid over the new bridge and pre-assembled track laid. On 18th December the old running line was slewed to the new line and the first train crossed the new bridge. After track-lifting, the work began on 22nd March, 1961 of dismantling the original bridge and finally on 14th May, the Exmouth Junction 45 ton steam crane No. DS 1580 lifted the 10 girders on to three bogie bolster wagons which were then propelled to Topsham by '700' class 0-6-0 No. 30691. The new bridge allowed heavier locomotives to work to Exmouth.

Immediately beyond the viaduct, Odam's Siding, situated at 5 m. 08 ch. and 22.8 chains in length, trailed left to a fertiliser factory. A key on the single line tablet unlocked the ground frame. The siding was worked by a special trip with an 'O2' class locomotive as this was the only type allowed due to weight restrictions, though the more usual motive power within the siding was block and tackle attached to steel posts beside the track.* On its return to Topsham it propelled the train with the brake van leading, the man in charge signalling by flag for the whole distance, speed being limited to six miles an hour. The train was brought to a stand before reaching the foot crossing situated at the south end of the station so that the guard could alight and protect the pedestrian crossing. Odam's Siding was taken out of use on 25th February, 1940. On the Exton marshes, 'cast' sheep were sometimes spotted by locomotive crews, who would inform the next station in order that the farmer could be contacted.

Woodbury Road (5 m. 67 ch.), was some two miles from Woodbury village so from 15th September, 1958 the station was appropriately renamed Exton after the nearer hamlet. On the east side of the line the original low platform has a concrete standard height extension at its northern end, giving it a total length of 429 feet. The station buildings were once hung with slates and the station master's house has become a private residence following a brief venture as a restaurant, and houses are now built on what was the station yard. At the station and to the south, stone pitching protects the line from the tidal estuary. The two sidings, which were worked from a ground frame released by electric tablet, catered for local requirements including domestic coal. They were closed

* *Industrial Locomotives of South Western England.* Edited by R. Hateley.

57

A down train arriving at Woodbury Road, c. 1905.   *Author's Collection*

A view from May 1970, the station was by this time known as Exton.   *John R. Bonser*

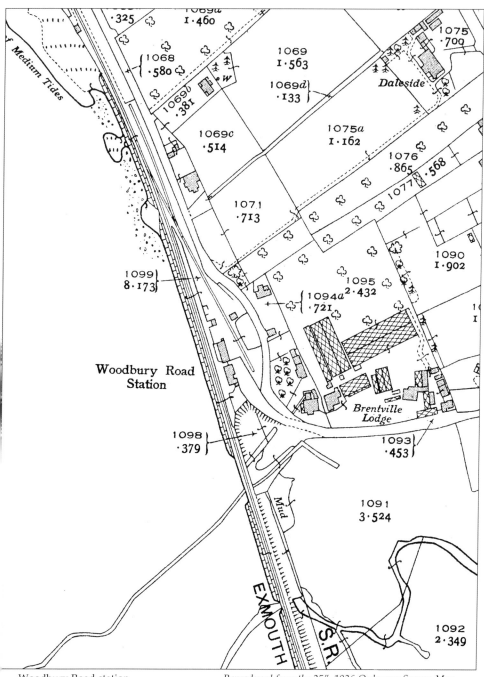

Woodbury Road station.   *Reproduced from the 25", 1936 Ordnance Survey Map*

Exton station as seen from the road, 31st May, 1970.   *John R. Bonser*

Exton, looking in the up direction showing the estuarial mud flat to the left, 18th July, 1989.
Note the extended higher platform at the up end.   *Author*

to traffic on 6th March, 1961, but retained for two camping coaches until lifted on 19th February, 1965.

The station is pleasantly situated beside the estuary with views across to Exminster and Powderham. Lympstone Commando station can be seen less than half a mile away from the end of the platform. At one time Woodbury Road had a station master and two signalmen, but by the 1920s it was staffed by two grade 1 porters responsible to the Topsham station master who travelled down on one train and returned on the next with the takings to put in the Topsham safe. All cash from the branch was placed in a leather bag bearing the name of the station from which it originated. A cash box measuring about 2 ft cube was chained to the brake column of the guard's van of the 8.00 am up from Exmouth and as it arrived at each station, the money bag was pushed through a flap in the top of the box. It was taken to the chief cashier at Exeter Central who held the key to unlock the box. The empty bags were returned to the various stations later that same day. Woodbury Road was busy during World War II, the coal and NAAFI supplies for the Marine camp arriving by rail, while on Saturdays as many as 250 tickets could be issued to the Marines.

In September 1960 serious flooding occurred when the stream which came down from Woodbury was so full that Bridge No. 16 could not take all the water, some of which followed the embankment to Bridge No. 15, immediately south of Woodbury Road station, where it damaged the concrete plinth. This was done on Friday 30th September, but trains were not stopped until lunch time on Monday 3rd October. Although one 'express' business service each way was diverted via Budleigh Salterton and Sidmouth Junction, all other trains from Exeter were reversed at Topsham and a connecting bus service run between Topsham and Exmouth. Following emergency repairs, normal service was resumed on 5th October, a 5 mph restriction being imposed. Subsequently two piers built from sleepers accommodated a replacement bridge brought from Lapford on the North Devon line (this line with a bridge for double track was never widened) and placed beside the original Bridge No. 15. On Sunday 5th March, 1961, after the old bridge had been removed during the night, the abutments were prepared by concrete bearing blocks being placed in position by 45 ton steam crane No. DS 1580 and hauled by 'N' class 2-6-0 No. 31841. This crane, together with 10 ton crane No. DS 1722, lifted the 28 ton bridge into position. Track laying and ballasting were completed before the arrival of the first train of the day, the 2.55 pm from Exmouth.

On the left of the line which now becomes level for a mile, can be seen Commando training equipment, before Lympstone Commando station (6 m. 23 ch.) which serves exclusively the Commando Training Centre, Royal Marines. Construction on the east side of the line commenced on 26th January, 1976. The platform was the Weston Milton Halt former down platform, unused since that line was singled on 31st January, 1972. The first section of platform was in place on 23rd February, 1976 and the task completed on the 27th. The shelter was erected on 9th March. The halt opened on 3rd May. The platform is 224 feet in length and long enough to accommodate a three-car dmu. Enamel notices state 'Only persons having business at CTCRM may alight'. Except for a military guard post, there is no booking office, but at busy periods during the day a

The 4.09 pm Exmouth-Exeter Central train calls at the new station of Lympstone Commando to pick up visitors attending the military tattoo, 24th July, 1976.   *S.P. Derek*

Lympstone Commando, view looking 'down'. Commando buildings are on the left; *c.* 1978.
   Lens of Sutton

conductor-guard with a portable ticket machine mans the station.

The gradient then rises at 1 in 122 for just over ¼ mile easing to 1 in 293 before reaching Lympstone station (7 m. 28 ch.) through a cutting spanned by an overbridge. At one time a trailing siding could be seen before reaching the station, which had a goods loop and one short siding serving a cattle dock. The single platform, on the western side of the line, is the original length of 323 feet, and had a brick building with narrow awning, while a small timber parcels and goods shed adjoined. The signal box was originally opposite this platform, but a new 12-lever box in the ticket office in the southern end of the station building was opened on 29th September, 1929 and closed 16th September, 1962, goods facilities having been withdrawn on 4th April, 1960. After the station building was boarded up in 1965, the larger parcels shed remained as a waiting shelter until demolition of all buildings in December 1976, when replaced by a modern bus stop-style shelter under the refurbishing programme. Stone flower containers and hanging baskets make the station quite attractive. The station was renamed Lympstone Village from 13th May, 1991.

In the 1920s Lympstone was staffed by a station master, clerk, two signalmen and a porter-signalman. Before unstaffing, it had two signalmen responsible to the Exmouth station master who supplied clerical assistance at peak periods. It dealt with general traffic including domestic coal. Tanks for cleaning mussels were sited near this fishing village and cockles and mussels despatched by rail, but the traffic died out by 1939. The platform ends on a three-arch viaduct which carries the line across the village. The viaduct is of red brick as are all the original bridges on the line. Its centre arch is used as a decorator's store.

After a short length of level track the line gradually descends for the remaining 1½ miles to Exmouth, paralleled by a public footpath, the retention of which was defended at the time of the line's construction. Its maintenance still causes problems as it is subject to erosion by the sea. A mile outside Exmouth a painted fixed distant board, which in January 1988 replaced the branch's last semaphore signal, gives plenty of warning of the terminus. At 8 m. 65 ch. was Warren's Siding, later owned by the East Devon Brick & Tile Company. Inspected by the Board of Trade on 29th September, 1884, it was taken out of use in May 1960. it made a facing connection on the down side and therefore was worked from Exmouth in a manner similar to Odam's Siding from Topsham. Only 'O2' class locomotives were permitted to enter the siding which was unlocked with the single line tablet key.

When Henry Lovatt & Sons were carrying out the contract for building a line to Budleigh Salterton, their temporary line crossed the single track main line at Exmouth just the Lympstone side of the leading station turnouts. To ensure the safety of LSWR trains, trap points and ground signals were provided on the temporary line on either side of the main line to control the crossing. the position of the LSWR down home signal was slightly altered. The new trap points were interlocked between the tablet instrument at Lympstone so that a tablet could not be taken out for a train from Lympstone to Exmouth while the points were set for the crossing. Major J.W. Pringle inspected this layout on 27th September, 1901.

Exmouth's present station (9 m. 32 ch.) is its third. A modern brick-built structure opened on 2nd May, 1976, it has a single platform 481 feet in length. The

Lympstone with the River Exe beyond, viewed *c.* 1904. The goods shed on the right was later converted to a waiting room. There is an interesting display of posters to be seen.

Lens of Sutton

The token is exchanged at Lympstone from BR Standard type '3' 2-6-2T No. 82013 as it works the 11.45 am Exmouth to Exeter Central, 2nd September, 1959.   *H.B. Priestley*

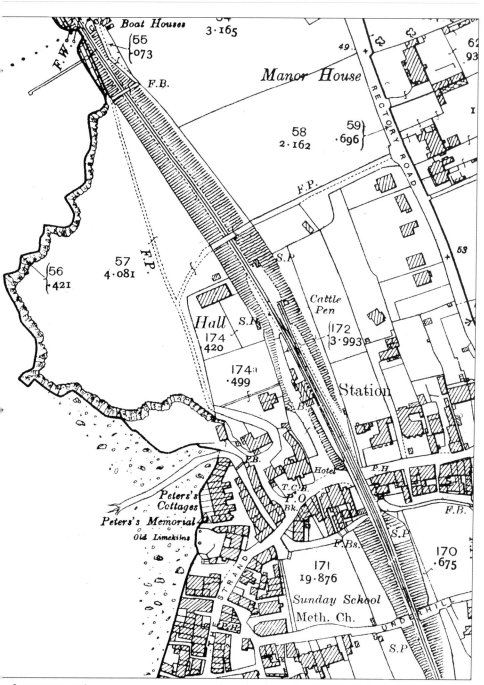

Lympstone station.

Reproduced from the 25″, 1933 Ordnance Survey Map

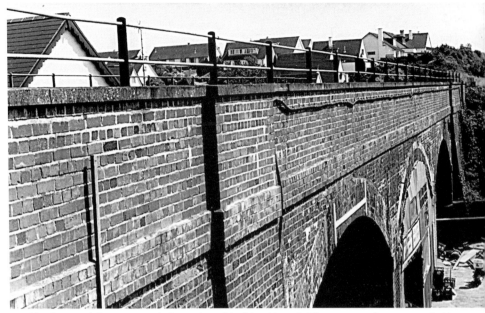

The three-arch Lympstone viaduct, viewed looking 'down'. The centre arch was occupied by a decorator, 17th July, 1989.   *Author*

Ivatt class '2MT' 2-6-2T No. 41307 is seen pulling away from Lympstone station with the 12.55 pm Exeter Central-Exmouth train on 15th June, 1958.   *S.C. Nash*

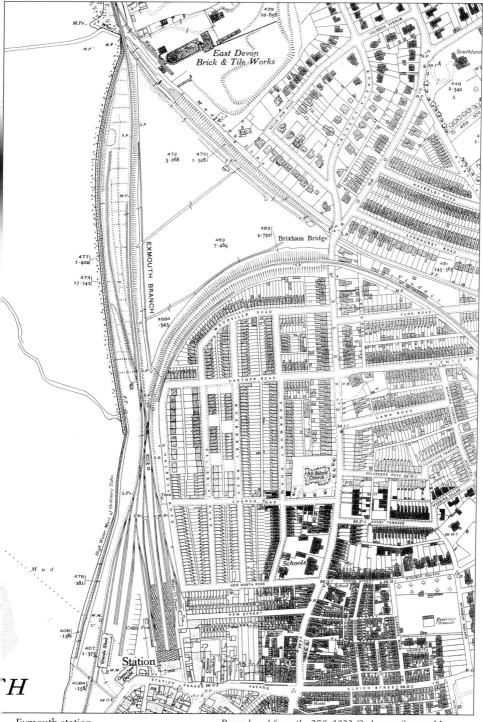

Exmouth station.

Reproduced from the 25″, 1933 Ordnance Survey Map

Exmouth: 'M7' class 0-4-4T No. 133 on the left with a train to Exeter Central; the train to Tipton St John's is at the right. Two Wall's 'Stop me and buy one' tricycles can be seen on the right-hand platform. Note the palms and water crane between the platforms. *Lens of Sutton*

A fine general view of Exmouth station from the signal box, with 'M7' class No. 30676, *left*, 13th October, 1959. *R.C. Riley*

original station building, suitably converted from two private houses, was situated about 300 feet further south and frontaged on to Imperial Road. It had an island platform with run-round loop, to the east of which was a turntable and engine shed, while to the west was a goods shed and three sidings. The passenger platform had a screen on its seaward side to protect passengers from the wind.

The opening of the Budleigh Salterton line on 1st June, 1903 which reduced the Waterloo to Exmouth mileage from 182¼ miles via Exeter Central to 175¾ miles via Tipton St John's, also created additional traffic which outstripped the capacity of the original station. The first alterations were inspected by Major Pringle on 21st January, 1910 when he checked new works at the south end of the station yard. The facing connection on the down platform road leading to the Quay branch had been removed, while the loop points had been brought back to within a working distance, 250 yds, of the station signal box. At the same time track circuiting had been installed between the down starting and down advanced starting signals, while the facing point bolt at the south end of the loop was electrically detected. The 23-lever frame now had four spare levers.

To the envy of Exeter, in 1924 a new station was built in red brick on a granite plinth, this 4-bay, 2-storey block flanked by single-storey bay wings. The parcels office was on the left of the main block and the booking office on the right. A metal canopy sheltered the entrances. The former dwelling house building was only demolished when the new terminal building was completed, its site forming a forecourt used by local taxi operators. The station master lived in a flat above the offices which included a spacious combined booking hall and general waiting room served by two ticket windows, one mainly for summer enquiries and reservations, opposite which was a wall display of train departure times in separate enamelled figures. On the east side of the roofed concourse were well-appointed gentlemen's conveniences, while on the opposite side was W.H. Smith & Son's bookstall which was transferred to the centre of the concourse about 1960, replacing a refreshment kiosk. On 4th February, 1974 the bookstall was taken over by E. Prior & Company, only to be finally closed on 2nd October.

Returning to the events of 50 years before the new enlarged layout costing £70,000 was brought into use on 20th July, 1924 when the two new platforms were added to the west. The lengths of platforms 1 to 4 were 607, 568, 568 and 614 feet respectively. The platform numbers were completely reversed on 2nd June, 1927, No. 1 becoming No. 4 and No. 2 becoming No. 3. Platforms 1 and 4 had run-round loops and were used principally for arrivals, locomotives running round and shunting stock into one of the centre platforms in order to leave the outer platforms clear for the next arrival. Alternatively, after running round, a return departure could be made either within six minutes of arrival, or after a longer layover, dependent on the timetable. The spur at the buffer stop end of the platform was only long enough to hold a tank engine; while there, it could take water from the adjacent column. Platforms 2 and 3 were occasionally used for arrivals involving the use of a turnover engine, or double shunt movement to an outer platform, and were served by a single water column sited just beyond the Exeter end of the roofed section, about six coach lengths from the buffer stops. The intervening six-foot between the platform lines was beautified with palm trees and shrubs.

Frank Love on the balcony of Exmouth signal box, *c.* 1960. *Author's Collection*

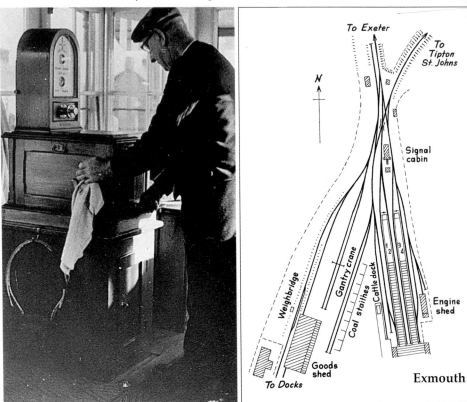

Above, left: Frank Love operating the single line tablet machine in Exmouth signal box *c.* 1960. Pouches with large handles hang on the left. *Author's Collection*

Above, right: Track plan of Exmouth *c.* 1960. *David Gould*

A view from the 11.45 am Exmouth-Exeter Central train on 2nd September, 1959, as it leaves Exmouth station. the train is headed by BR Standard class '3' 2-6-2T No. 82013. The sharply curving line to the right of the signal is for Tipton St John's. *H.B. Priestley*

A 1960s view along the platform at Exmouth as BR Standard class '4' 2-6-4T No. 80039 runs round its train comprising Set No. 152. *M. Daly*

The exterior of Exmouth station in January 1924, with scaffolding poles marking the site of the site of the new station.   The long notice board on the wall on the left advertises the LSWR's delivery and collection agents C. Hayne & Son.   *Author's Collection*

The exterior of Exmouth station photographed on 18th August, 1978.   *Author*

The 1924 alterations also included a new 70-lever signal box which was situated conveniently between the convergence of the lines from platforms 1 and 2, and 3 and 4. It had overhanging balconies at each site of the southern end from which the signalman could pass the single line tablet to or from the fireman without having to descend the steps. As simultaneous departures or arrivals were possible from both the Exeter and Budleigh lines, the signalman occasionally had to move quickly across the balcony. An indicator on each home signal showed the arrival platform number to incoming trains and prepared the fireman for his tablet delivery. Safety features included track circuits and an illuminated track diagram. The four LSWR lower quadrant starting signals on each of the two gantries at the end of the platforms were replaced by upper quadrant arms about 1961.

Exmouth, the terminal for both the Exeter and Budleigh line services, was a busy station. Exeter, the county town of Devon, was the centre for employment, education and shopping and ever since the 1880s the number of passengers commuting to Exeter has been increasing. The line was particularly active at rush hours when to find an empty compartment was rare. In 1958 for instance, the two-coach 7.38 am from Tipton St John's could be full leaving Littleham and on arriving at Exmouth at 8.7, the majority of its passengers would cross the platform and change into the 8.10 to Exeter, already filling with commuters trying not to mix with children bound for Exeter schools. In the opposite direction Exmouth attracted a smaller commuting flow arriving mainly at 8.44 am with pupils bound for the Exmouth Grammar and Secondary Schools. Shoppers, some with prams, and other travellers featured on the later trains, while summer weekdays would see train loads of holidaymakers departing during the morning and arriving from mid-day, intermingling with the regular local traffic.

A ticket collector's kiosk served platforms 1 and 4 and each platform had lattice gates, kept closed and only opened 10 minutes before the departure of a train. A poster at each read: This barrier will be closed immediately before the train is due to leave to ensure punctual departure'. A green enamel notice read: 'Front 2 coaches for St James' Park and Lympstone stations', while going down, the 'halt' coaches were at the rear.

Nos. 1, 2 and 3 platform roads were taken out of use on 20th December, 1968 together with the run-round loop to platform No. 4, this being superfluous as all regular trains on the branch were diesel-multiple-units. On the rare occasion when a locomotive-hauled special now uses the branch, a locomotive has to be provided at each end.

In the 1920s, Exmouth was staffed by a station master; two booking clerks; two ticket collectors, (one of which was Harrison, the guard of the train involved in the 1906 accident at Salisbury); two platform foremen and three porters; while the goods depot was looked after by a chief goods clerk; two goods clerks; two checkers; two goods porters; two shunters and three porter-guards. There were also two signalmen and a porter-signalman. Exmouth's last station master retired on 1st February, 1966, the station being placed under an inspector; the station was partially unstaffed from 6th May, 1968. Today the booking office has restricted opening hours, but when closed, a railman is on duty with a ticket machine.

Exmouth shed on 21st June, 1957 with 'M7' class 0-4-4T No. 30044 in view.   *John R. Bonser*

A view of the depot from the station platform in August 1962, with Ivatt class '2' 2-6-2T No. 41320 and a sister engine on shed.   *T.J. Edgington*

An accident occurred to the Exmouth station master, Walter Shrimpton, on the evening of 15th August, 1871, when he visited the jeweller's shop of a friend of his, William Maynard, situated in The Strand. Shrimpton inquired, 'Aren't you afraid of being robbed?' and Maynard replied jokingly, 'Oh no, I've got a very good friend here' and so saying, he pulled open a drawer, took out what he thought was an unloaded pistol, pointed it at Shrimpton and pulled the trigger. There was an explosion and the station master dropped dead.

Enlargement of the site in the 1920s brought an increase in the number of goods sidings to seven, as well as a new brick-built goods shed opened on 21st July, 1924, which had an extensive concrete platform for dealing with merchandise, four delivery openings and overhead cranes. A gantry crane in the yard transferred containers between wagon and lorry. Two coal sidings, one with staithes, were kept for domestic coal requirements and a cattle dock was provided. The goods shed closed on 4th December, 1967, first becoming a skateboard rink, then later a sports hall within the new Exmouth Sports Centre which included a swimming pool; the remainder of the former goods yard is used as a car park and terminal facilities for the bus station.

The goods delivery agent at Exmouth was Mr Haynes, the family holding the position for the whole period the station dealt with freight traffic. When the line was opened in 1861, Frederick Haynes gave up being a carrier between Exmouth and Exeter and acted as LSWR goods delivery agent, delivering from Budleigh Salterton when the line was opened there. Exmouth also had an outside porter, a non-railway servant who as well as carrying passengers' luggage, would assist commercial travellers who took their samples in large hampers called 'skips'. The outside porter arranged to meet these travellers and went round the town with them. An outside porter's truck was about 6 feet in length, with three wheels in front and two behind.

Exmouth in the late 1970s soon after completion of the new terminal building.
Lens of Sutton

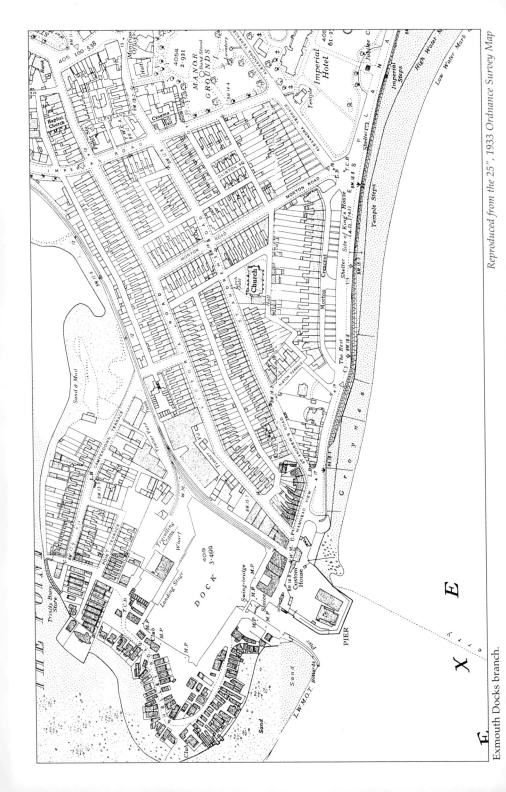

Reproduced from the 25", 1933 Ordnance Survey Map

Exmouth Docks branch.

Chapter Seven

The Exmouth Docks Line

In 1863 a Bill was put forward to authorise the Exmouth Pier Company to construct and maintain a dock and railway. A dock was necessary to avoid vessels having to anchor in the Bight and discharge their cargo into lighters. On 10th December, 1863 a deputation from the scheme's promoters saw Archibald Scott, General Manager of the LSWR, and gained his support, as a rival project was being put forward the other side of the Exe backed by the South Devon Railway and this threatened traffic on the Exmouth branch. An Act of 29th July, 1864, 27 & 28 Vict. cap. 319, authorised construction of a basin and allowed the Dock Company to raise a capital of £60,000 and enter into a working agreement with the LSWR and E&E for operating a siding. This was to run from the west end of the goods yard to the Docks, a distance of 21.4 chains to the Docks entrance, where two sidings ran to the south side and two to the east. Freight receipts went to a joint fund, paying the Docks Company 6*d.*, 1*s.* or 1*s.* 6*d.* per ton carried according to the class of goods, any excess going to the LSWR.

The Docks were constructed by converting a natural U-shaped indent of the shore known as 'Shellpit'. In January 1865 Messrs Jackson of London began work, the Docks being opened in 1868. They could accommodate ships up to 750 tons deadweight, 180 ft length, 28 ft beam and approximately 10 ft 6 in. draft. Very nearly all traffic was inwards, quite a proportion of it going on by rail to the branch stations. At one time all Exmouth's coal came by sea and a coaling staithe was provided with cranes and gantries. Installed in 1933, these gantries were self-propelled on single rails and straddled the dock siding for approximately 100 yards. The two grabs enabled a pair of colliers to be unloaded at a time. Other traffic was timber, wood pulp, grain, fertiliser, cider apples and apple juice from France for Whiteways, Whimple. Herring fishing was good in 1881 and one January night almost 40 tons of fish were landed. A few days later, 63 tons of fish were caught, two special trains taking them to London. Special herring trains were an occasional feature, but they died out completely in the mid-1920s.

Trucks were propelled to the Docks as no suitable run-round facilities were available there, a flagman seeing them safely across the ungated crossings over the lane leading to the King George's Recreation Ground and over the crossing at Camperdown Terrace. Some wagons were retained for internal use only and carried the stencilled instruction: 'Only to be used between Exmouth Docks & Exmouth station'. Trains were restricted to a speed of 4 miles an hour. At one time two trains ran daily but latterly trains only ran as required. The private siding agreement was terminated and the line closed on 2nd December, 1967, the line being taken out of use on 10th March, 1968, the same day as the goods yard at Exmouth. The Docks ceased to be used for commercial shipping from 1990.

The line was subject to weight restrictions. In the summer of 1895 a Manning, Wardle 0-6-0 saddle tank engine No. 458 *Jumbo* was transferred to Exmouth Junction for use on the branch but on 17th January the following year it was involved in a shunting accident at Topsham in a snowstorm, was dispatched to Nine Elms works and five months later had its firebox condemned and was withdrawn from service.* Shanks 0-4-0ST No. 110 *Ritzebuttel*, purchased by the

* *LSWR Locomotives: The Adams Classes*, D.C. Bradley.

77

The docks line originally extended beyond the Customs House, *left*, as can be seen in this World War I view.
The Devon Dock, Pier & Steamship Co. Ltd

This postcard view is believed to be post-World War II. A number of wagons can be seen on the quayside.
G. Pridmore Collection

The Harbour, Exmouth 12638

A view across the basin at Exmouth. The sidings are busy on the eastern side of the dock, *right*, and a BR mineral wagon is visible near the coal depot on the northern quay.

G. Pridmore Collection

Ivatt class '2' 2-6-2T No. 41307 is seen with a single wagon near Camperdown Terrace, 24th September, 1958.

Pamlin Prints

Right: A lorry is seen blocking one of the sidings on the eastern side of the basin as it stands alongside German vessel *Hedwig Hennig* of Hamburg in June 1965. Wagons stand to the right.

The Devon Dock, Pier & Steamship Co. Ltd

Below: Ivatt class '2' 2-6-2T No. 41309 crosses Camperdown Terrace with the early morning trip from the docks, 5th June, 1961.

S.P. Derek

LSWR in 1879 from the contractor Alfred Giles for use on the Royal Pier tramway, Southampton, shunted to Exmouth Docks in May 1911. The heaviest locomotives allowed over the branch were Adams' 'O2' class tank engines, the only type permitted to work over the weighbridge near Exmouth goods shed until 1960 when class '2' 2-6-2Ts were authorised. Following the withdrawal of steam, D63XX diesel-hydraulic engines (later class '22') worked the line.

A short walk from the Dock sidings and adjacent to the landing stage steps by the narrow entrance channel, was the booking office of the Starcross Ferry where, during the 1950s, brown and cream enamelled Western Region-headed publicity boards were evident. 'The right of ferry from Exmouth to the opposite shore at the mouth of the River Exe' was traceable back to 1122 when this privilege, among others, was conferred on the Priory of Sherborne. In 1265 the ferry right was transferred to the City of Exeter in exchange for other interests.

It was the coming of the broad gauge South Devon Railway on the west bank of the River Exe that extended the ferry's importance and in 1844 Exeter Corporation sold it to the SDR for £1,000. Licensed rowing boats endeavoured to connect, unless they became stuck on the estuarial sandbanks, with trains at Starcross station. One consequence of the opening of the Exeter & Exmouth Railway was the diminution of the ferry's traffic.

About 1890 the first steam ferry was introduced to this crossing and around 1898 the Exmouth & Great Western Steam Ferry Company Limited sold the service to the Devon Dock, Pier and Steamship Company Limited, owners of Exmouth Dock. Through booking facilities were offered to and from the GWR, the LSWR losing this revenue. For rather more than the first half of the 20th century the ferry enjoyed a heyday, its service being included in the appropriate railway timetables. For example they appeared in the GWR Passenger Timebook for 1899, the WR and SR timetables during the 1950s, and the British Rail timetable for the 1980s.

Passenger traffic was customarily thin during the winter months, partly offset by the GWR/WR's parcel traffic until this was concentrated at Exeter St David's during the Beeching years. By then the passenger service had become a summer-only operation and in 1981 the Devon Dock, Pier and Steamship Company Limited relinquished its ownership to a succession of local ferry operators which still provide a summer ferry and river cruise service.

The dock basin has frozen as two wagons stand at the quayside in January 1940.
The Devon Dock, Pier & Steamship Co. Ltd

A contractor's locomotive at Exmouth, *c.* 1861.   *Author's Collection*

Adams '380' class 4-4-0 No. 382 at Exmouth, *c.* 1900.   *Dr T.F. Budden*

Chapter Eight

Steam Locomotives

As mentioned before, the first turn to Exmouth was worked by No. 36 *Comet,* a 'Sussex' class 2-2-2 well-tank engine. Nos. 4 *Locke,* 19 *Briton* and 20 *Princess* (members of the same class), ended their days on the Exmouth branch, being scrapped in 1873, 1876 and 1871 respectively. 2-2-2 well-tanks of the 'Tartar' class recorded on the branch from September to December 1867 were Nos. 2 *Tartar,* 12 *Jupiter,* 13 *Orion,* 33 *Phoenix,* joined the following year by Nos. 17 *Queen* and 18 *Albert* the other two members of the class which had been working on the Lymington branch. All these engines were withdrawn between 1871 and 1874. No. 76 *Firefly* was damaged on 11th October, 1865 when a faulty point at Woodbury Road caused it to be derailed. Tender engines displaced from main line duties also appeared on the line. These were Rothwell 2-2-2 engines Nos. 73 *Fireball,* 77 *Wildfire,* 79 *Harpy* and 97 *Pegasus,* and Fairbairn locomotives of the same wheel arrangement Nos. 64 *Acheron* and 65 *Achilles* which were used before being scrapped in 1872 and 1871.

In April 1861 'Nelson' class 2-4-0 well-tank No. 144 *Howe* was transferred to Exeter for the opening of the Exmouth line, but was moved away by 1875. In the mid-1870s Exeter had Beattie standard 2-4-0 well tank engines Nos. 195/6/9, 244/5/6/9 and 251 for various duties including the service to Exmouth. 'Volcano' class 2-4-0 No. 11 *Minerva* worked all the branch passenger services in March 1878. Six rebuilt standard well tanks Nos. 44 *Pluto,* 257, 266, 298, 314 and 329 were shedded at Exmouth Junction in the mid-1890s for working the branch. (No. 298, later BR No. 30587, and No. 314, BR No. 30585, are both preserved.) Most individual engines only operated over the line for a year or two before being transferred elsewhere, but one member of the class was still active on the branch in 1919.

'Ilfracombe Goods' engine 0-6-0 No. 301 was allocated to Exmouth in June 1881, and Nos. 0283/4 and 0393 were shedded at Exmouth Junction in the early 1900s for the branch goods train, taking over this duty from Beyer, Peacock double-frame 0-6-0 goods engine No. 0288. Adams 'B4' class 0-4-0 tank engine No. 92 was observed on a goods in May 1892, but it is not known whether this was a regular feature. Adams '0380' class 4-4-0 engines Nos. 0381/3/4 were stabled at Exmouth Junction early in 1905 and put in an appearance on the branch goods. In March 1901 Adams 'G6' 0-6-0 tank engines Nos. 270/4/5/8/9 were shedded at Exmouth Junction and among other duties worked goods trains to Exmouth.

Telford, a 2-4-0 engine built by George England in 1861 for the Engineer's Department, spent the autumn of 1892 removing soil from an earth slip on the branch. In 1892 Beattie '348' class 4-4-0 No. 351 appeared at Exmouth. Adams '415' class 4-4-2 tank engines worked from the 1880s, but not the older '46' class Adams 4-4-0 tanks which were prohibited because of their greater axle weight. In 1914 three 4-4-2 tank engines were shedded at Exmouth Junction, one normally sub-shedded at Lyme Regis, the other two being employed on the

'O2' class 0-4-4T No. 224 and Adams '415' class 4-4-2T No. 0125 (right) at Exmouth Junction shed, *c.* 1932. *Lens of Sutton*

'O2' class No. 30232 at Exmouth shed, 2nd September, 1951. *R.A. Lumber*

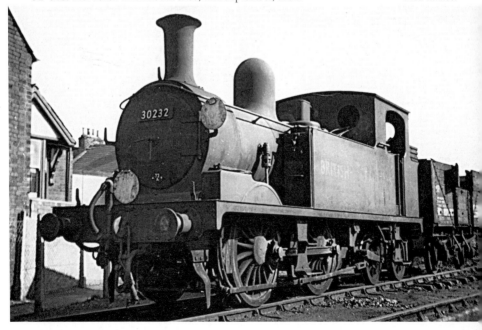

Exmouth branch. In the early year of Grouping Nos. 0125, 0486, 0520/1 were stabled at Exmouth Junction for these workings.

'Terrier' 0-6-0 tank engine No. 734, purchased from the LBSCR for hauling the Lyme Regis trains, prior to the opening of this line worked, among other duties, the Exeter to Exmouth goods in the spring of 1903 and became derailed in sidings at Topsham on 12th June of that year. Following the opening of the Lyme Regis branch, in winter either No. 734 or No. 735 was sub-shedded at Lyme, the engines being exchanged weekly, the spare often being utilised on goods trains to Exmouth, while between the early months of 1908 and the autumn, this class, having been found unsuited to the Lyme Regis branch, saw No. 735 transferred to Exmouth for local shunting and working the Dock line.

0-4-4 tank engines of the 'T1' class were too heavy for the Exmouth line, but similar smaller engines of the 'O2' class were light enough and a report to Adams dated September 1893 showed the 'O2' class as being well-suited for the duty, burning 16 per cent less fuel than the Beattie well tanks in addition to suffering 34 per cent less failures. In March 1900 Nos. 179 and 187 were shedded at Exmouth Junction for branch operation and in 1904-6 Nos. 209 and 231, together with '0415' class Nos. 0520/3 and 0107, were working most of the services, Nos. 179 and 231 being recorded in 1911. About the year 1932 'O2' class Nos. 178, 181, 191/8, 203/7/8, 214, 228, 231/2/5 operated the Exeter-Exmouth-Sidmouth services. In July 1939, Exmouth Junction had Nos. 181, 199, 224/5/8 for the branch, one of these locomotives being sub-shedded at Exmouth for shunting at the Docks and also at Topsham. During World War II Nos. 193, 224, 230/2 worked on the Exmouth branch. When 'M7' 0-4-4 tank engines took over the services, one member of the 'O2' class was still retained for the Exmouth Dock and Topsham Quay lines as 'M7s' were too heavy for these duties. In 1955 an 'O2' still hauled the evening pick-up goods from Exmouth, returning with the 9.20 pm passenger Exeter to Exmouth.

Although tank engines usually headed passenger trains, in the period from 1904 to 1906 an Adams 0-6-0 of the '0395' class, usually Nos. 027/8, 0168, 0172, 0395 or 0404, worked the 5.30 pm Exeter (Queen Street) to Exmouth.

Following the removal of the 'M7s' restriction between Topsham and Exmouth in July 1932, Nos. 37, 41/4/5, 133, 247, 356, 375, 669 and 671 were transferred to Exmouth Junction for the Exmouth services. By mid-1937 the allocation had been changed to Nos. 24, 34/7/9, 44, 123/4, 133, 256, 321/3, 356, 374/5/6/7, 669 and 671. Their workings, among other duties, included two engines Exeter to Exmouth; five Exeter to Exmouth thence Sidmouth; two engines Exeter to Exmouth thence Sidmouth Junction. Motor-fitted 'M7s' Nos. 27, 46 and 55 ran to Exmouth when not required on the Seaton branch.

Drummond 'H13' class steam railcars Nos. 5 and 6 were used for the service which began between Exeter and Topsham on 1st June, 1908, 'C14' class 2-2-0 tank engines Nos. 736 and 740 sharing duties with the railcars. Subsequently railcars Nos. 12 and 13 were noted, but by the summer of 1914 the service was operated by Nos. 6 and 14. As the cars were scrapped, motor trains replaced them.

On 23rd July, 1952 LMR class '2MT' 2-6-2T No. 41314 made a series of trial runs between Exeter and Exmouth with seven coaches, the maximum 'M7'

'M7' class 0-4-4T No. 376 stands at Exmouth Junction shed waiting for the road to Central station to head a train to Exmouth, *c.* 1947.   *Roger Venning*

'M7' class 0-4-4T No. 30374 heads the 6.12 pm Exeter Central-Exmouth train near Woodbury Road on 15th June, 1958.   *S.C. Nash*

loading, but although its time-keeping was exemplary, it did not perform noticeably better than the older class. It was joined by Nos. 41313/5. BR Standard class '3' 2-6-2T No. 82011 produced a much superior performance, accelerating well up the in 97/128 bank from Topsham towards Exeter with loads of up to 7 bogies. By October Nos. 82010/1/3/7/8/9 monopolised the service, backed by No. 41314 and 'M7s' Nos. 30023/5, 30045, 30667/9. BR Standard class '3' Nos. 82022/3/4/5 appeared later. A curiosity in 1957 was a Drummond 'T9' 4-4-0 occasionally heading the branch goods.

In 1959 the following members of the 'M7' class were still at work on the Exmouth line: Nos. 30023/4/5, 30323, 30667/9, 30670/6. Nos. 30024/5 appeared occasionally on the 8.50 am Exmouth-Exeter Central and the 9.22 am Exeter Central-Exmouth, No. 30025 being the last engine of the class to make an appearance on the branch when it worked these trains on 20th April, 1963. In 1959 Ivatt class '2' 2-6-2 tank engines Nos. 41284, 41299, 41306/7/8, 41318, 41320/2/3 were seen on the branch.

BR class '2' 2-6-2 tank engines Nos. 84020-3 arrived at Exmouth Junction in May 1961 from the Eastern Section of the Southern Region, but their stay was short for they were transferred to the London Midland Region during September and October of the same year.

In June 1962 No. 80035 was the first of 12 BR Standard class '4' 2-6-4Ts to arrive at Exmouth Junction from various sheds and Regions, these engines replacing the 82XXX tanks, although it was some seven months before all the newcomers arrived these being Nos. 80035-43/59/64/67.

Although latterly freight trains were worked by the branch passenger engines, occasionally BR class '4' or SR 'N' class 2-6-0s appeared, the latter being used on stone trains from Budleigh Salterton. 'S15' 4-6-0 engines sometimes appeared on goods trains from Exeter to Exmouth. Steam locomotives on the Newcourt Sidings train were usually an 'N15', 'H15', 'S15' 4-6-0, or Maunsell 2-6-0 or a Bulleid Pacific. During the winter months of 1959 to 1960, Western Region motive power stationed at Exmouth Junction occasionally appeared on the branch, an example being 0-6-0 pannier tank engine No. 3633 which was seen on 27th February, 1960. Although engines of the 'West Country' class did not normally work over the line, No. 21C115 *Exmouth* was christened at the town on 26th June, 1946, travelling via Tipton to avoid bridge restrictions. O.V.S. Bulleid, its designer, was an Exmothian. Following the rebuilding of the River Clyst viaduct, the restriction on the use of light Pacifics was lifted in 1960.

Exmouth locomotive depot was a sub-shed of Exmouth Junction. The original locomotive shed at Exmouth, which dated from the opening of the branch, was a one-road, single-ended building, access being across a 42 ft diameter turntable. As the original water tank was of limited capacity, in 1871 a second was built beside it. In 1926 the shed employed 19 men including eight pairs of drivers/firemen. In 1927 the SR erected a replacement shed of concrete blocks with a water tank on the roof at the far end. As the turntable was virtually unused, it was removed. Following Nationalisation in 1948 Exmouth Junction locomotives bore the BR shed code 72A. There were eight pairs of men at the Exmouth depot at its maximum, with three cleaners and four

'M7' class 0-4-4T No. 30676 stands in Exmouth shed yard on 13th October, 1959.   *R.C. Riley*

Ivatt class '2' 2-6-2T No. 41306 is seen at Exmouth on 10th October, 1959.   *R.C. Riley*

BR Standard class '3' 2-6-2T No. 82011 is seen approaching Lympstone with the 2.15 pm Exeter Central-Exmouth train on 15th June, 1958. *S.C. Nash*

BR Standard class '3' 2-6-2T No. 82017 is seen leaving Exmouth with the 1.45 pm to Exeter on 13th October, 1959. *R.C. Riley*

locomotives. The driver in charge of the depot always worked the middle shift. In 1960 the shed had an allocation of four engines, though individually they varied from day to day. It consisted of two class '3' 2-6-2 tank engines; one class '2' 2-6-2 tank locomotive and one 'M7' 0-4-4T. As there were no coaling facilities, each engine visited Exmouth Junction daily for this purpose and also any necessary examination, occasionally branch trains being double-headed to work an extra engine from Exmouth. A coal wagon was kept at Exmouth for topping up purposes.

Transferred to the Western Region in January 1963 the depot became 83D but was not officially so designated until the following September. Following closure on 4th November, 1963, the shed was demolished in the summer of 1967.

Headcodes

LSWR: diamond nearside mid-iron, disc offside mid-iron, on locomotives working Exmouth-Exeter Central. Disc on offside mid-iron for Exmouth-Tipton St John's.
SR: disc at chimney, Exmouth-Exeter Central, disc at centre of buffer-beam, Exmouth-Tipton St John's.

BR Standard class '4' No. 80067 runs round its train at Exmouth *c.* 1962.   *M. Daly*

Chapter Nine

Diesel Traction

In 1957 the Southern Region announced details of its plans which included diesel-electric traction for the East Devon branches, units to be based at Exmouth Junction in a new depot built in the 'V' between the main and branch lines, intimating that this work would be completed in 1959. It was envisaged that a 20-minute interval service would be operated between Budleigh Salterton-Exmouth-Exeter Central, a rebuilt Exton station incorporating an island platform, signal box and crossing loop as this was to have been the halfway point for the planned service. This imaginative scheme was postponed as a result of government economy restrictions and then abandoned when the area was taken over by the Western Region.

The first diesel-mechanical multiple unit appeared on 12th June, 1963 making two test runs in public service. Exmouth signal box had projecting balconies to facilitate passing the single line tablet while in motion, but with diesels, it was mandatory that they should stop. On 9th September, 1963 the Exmouth branch timetable was revised and the former 3- to 5-car dmu formations, in use since their introduction on 15th July, were replaced by 3-car sets only, both of the cross-country and suburban types. For business trains this provided insufficient accommodation until 27th January, 1964 when an additional trailer was added. The dmu service was based on Newton Abbot with the units on two-day diagrams, with 'empty' transfers between Central and St David's stations.

After 9th September, 1963 the only booked passenger steam workings to remain were the 8.20 am fast to Exeter and the return 5.49 pm slow, but steam still substituted when the occasional diesel failure occurred. Meanwhile the Budleigh branch saw its first dmu when an empty test run was made from Exeter to Exmouth via Sidmouth Junction and Tipton and back the same way on 27th June, 1963, followed by dmu operation of the 5.45 pm Exeter Central to Budleigh Salterton through service from 15th July. After 9th September the 4.00 pm and 5.20 pm Exmouth to Tipton and the return trains were replaced by 3-car dmus, while from 4th November 2-car suburban units appeared on nearly all of the services.

With the re-naming of Exmouth Junction Motive Power Depot to Exeter Running & Maintenance Depot caused by merging it with the WR St David's shed, the policy was to eliminate steam entirely from the depot by June 1965. The principal main line duties had already been relinquished to diesel power during August and September 1964 and it was now the turn of the Exmouth branch. Coincidental with splitting the long distance dmu workings to improve time-keeping and the progressive elimination of steam, the 8.20 am from Exmouth and the 5.45 pm Exeter Central to Budleigh Salterton and ancillary workings were finally replaced by dmus from 4th January, 1965. Only the 5.45 am Exmouth Junction Sidings and the 3.42 pm Exmouth freight remained steam-hauled. Steam's last duty on the freight services ceased on 24th May, 1965.

Class '118' dmu Set P464 with an Exmouth-Exeter St David's train at Exmouth Junction, 29th September, 1977.   *Col M.H. Cobb*

Two 3-car sets with P555 leading, comprising the 1.18 pm Exmouth-Exeter St David's seen here arriving at Lympstone on 16th August, 1978.   *Author*

During the next two decades the services were worked by various combinations of both suburban and cross-country two, or three, car sets which sported a variety of liveries. It was not until a suitably-designed replacement unit was built that the first generation dmus, by now having seen a quarter of century of service, could be considered for withdrawal. Following a few prototypes, the definitive vehicle was the lightweight four-wheeled class '142' 'Pacer' dmu, known in the West Country as a 'Skipper' and wearing a distinctive livery of chocolate and cream.

Developed by British Rail Engineering Limited and the Leyland Bus Company, each vehicle of the two-car unit was powered by a 162 ITW six-cylinder turbo-charged diesel engine. Set 142 015 first appeared on the branch on 15th October, 1985 with driver training trips, these continuing throughout the month. The class's first recorded use on a service train was 142 018 on 27th November, 1985. By mid-December the class covered failures of first generation dmus and entered regular public service on 20th January, 1986. Technical difficulties were encountered, particularly in relation to being identified on track circuits and so the 'Pacers' were temporarily withdrawn until 11th March, 1986. By 7th April, 1986 three class '142' diagrams were in operation covering the Barnstaple to Exmouth services, with full working from the beginning of the 12th May, 1986 timetable.

After barely 18 months in service, the West Country fleet of 13 twin units were found to be unsuitable due to a transmission failure, troublesome folding doors and flange wear, so were progressively withdrawn during the late autumn of 1987. One of their last duties was on the Exmouth branch when on Friday 27th November two sets worked the 8.43 pm Barnstaple to Exmouth and return. The last remaining four sets left Laira depot, Plymouth for Neville Hill, Leeds, on Monday 30th November, 1987 to join the rest of their 'Pacer' cousins in the Manchester and Yorkshire areas.

The 'Pacer' exercise involved the WR in an expenditure of £4½ million - each single unit cost £350,000 - and produced much unfavourable press comment since it occurred so soon after the initial welcoming publicity. Management scoured the country for the best of the older first generation dmus and brought classes '101', '108' and '121' from the Midland and Eastern Regions. These elderly sets, described publicly as 'Heritage Units' in view of their longevity of service, had to soldier on until 'Sprinter' dmus were deployed in the West of England.

Several rare workings were noted such as a Network South East-liveried class '117' 3-car dmu comprising Nos. 51366, 59518 and 51408 on 21st March, 1988. Class '150/2' Set No. 150 263 made a return trip to Exmouth on 7th July, 1988 for the benefit of Devon County Council's Transport Committee. A class '158' was tried on 13th September, 1990 and reappeared for Route Clearance Tests on 23rd February, 1992. Meanwhile the new class '155' 2-coach 'Sprinter' dmus made their progressive appearance on the branch from the commencement of the summer 1990 timetable, initially working the 8.02 pm Exeter St David's to Exmouth and return, Fridays and Saturdays excepted.

Following diagram changes by Regional Railways South Wales & West (the Western Region's successor), from 21st January, 1991, several services were

Rear of 6-car 1.18 pm Exmouth-St David's north of Lympstone, 16th August, 1978.   *Author*

Set P432 with car No. W51370 nearest the camera is seen at Exton with the 3.50 pm Exmouth-Exeter St David's train, 28th April, 1982.   *Tom Heavyside*

Class '142' dmu crossing the motorway link road near Digby, 9th September, 1987.

Stephen Cummins

Exmouth: Set P825 class '101' Nos. 51246/59118/53165 working the 1.45 pm to Exeter St David's, 21st July, 1989.

Author

Class '155' No. 155 329 is seen departing Exeter Central with the 2.14 pm Barnstaple-Exmouth service on 6th April, 1991. *Tom Heavyside*

A rear view of No. 150 261 at Digby & Sowton working the 11.54 am Exmouth to Paignton, 11th March, 1997. *Author*

worked by class '155' 'Sprinters' but from 8th July, 1991 no 'Sprinters' were diagrammed, all trains being of 2- or 3- car 'Heritage Units'. During the spring of 1992 deliveries of class '153' single railcars, converted from one vehicle of a class '155' twin, began to reappear concurrently with class '150/2' 2-car units. Although the old classes had been planned to be phased out during the preceding winter 1992-3 timetable, the 'Heritage' dmus lingered until 1993, Set T304 being recorded working six round trips over the branch on 24th June, 1993. Today the more luxurious 'Sprinter Express' 2-car dmus make occasional appearances and various combinations of all modern second generation dmu types can be seen either working alone or coupled with other classes. Early in 1994 class '159' units frequently appeared, while in January 1997, class '143' dmus, hitherto banned from the branch, were allowed to run 'in exceptional circumstances'. In March 1997 most workings were handled by class '150/2' and class '153' units.

The branch has at one time or another been used by most of the diesel-electric and diesel-hydraulic locomotives at work on the Western Region, including a High Speed Train, comprising two class '43' power cars and seven coaches.

A rear view of No. 153 380 at Digby & Sowton working the 12.20 pm Exeter St David's to Exmouth, 11th March, 1997. *Author*

'M7' class 0-4-4T No. 30676 at Exmouth station's platform 3, with a train to Exeter Central, c. 1952.

Chapter Ten

Coaching Stock

The *Exeter Flying Post*, 25th May, 1870 carried the complaint:

Tobacco smoking on railway carriages (says a correspondent) is still grievous. Railway companies have very properly provided smoking compartments; but very few smokers find their way to them. Our correspondent says he goes regularly to Exmouth by the bathing train; but has thus far in the season had the misfortune to get into a carriage where there have been three or four smokers. Perhaps those in the carriage are asked if they object to smoking? If one says he does he becomes the subject for ridicule by the smokers, who jib at him in a roundabout way to the end of the journey. This prevails to such an extent on the Exmouth line on Sunday mornings that many persons are deterred from availing themselves of the privilege of enjoying fresh air and a dip in the briny. Our correspondent thinks there is a great laxity on the part of the railway people, who instead of walking up and down the platform, nodding to Jack or Jim, to Mary or 'Tilda, and now and then shouting 'Any more for Exmouth' should seek to get the smokers together in the compartment for them, and not allow that carriage to be filled, as it very often is, by young women and boys. People going by train pop into any carriage, for the doors are generally opened, and this accounts for the smoking compartments being often filled to the exclusion of the smokers. The railway authorities will do a good service by causing a more active supervision than is now the case - at least with the bathing train to Exmouth. If a porter were stationed at each of the smoking compartments and were to say 'This is a smoking carriage', and not allow mere children to get into it, an evil would be remedied.

A memorial was sent to the LSWR Directors on 19th January, 1899 from residents of Exmouth complaining of antiquated and uncomfortable coaches on the Exmouth branch. They said that those of the first class were little, if at all better than the second class on the main line, while those of the second and third class were 'not only comfortless, but also for the most part repulsively dirty'.

In the 1930s the Exmouth branch old arc-roofed Panter non-lavatory sets were displaced by London, Brighton & South Coast and South Eastern & Chatham stock, a few loose coaches of the latter lasting until after World War II. These in turn were superseded by LSWR 56/58 ft lavatory two-coach sets and loose thirds designed by Warner. The 58-footers were the earlier 50 ft type lengthened by the SR. The 3-coach lavatory main line stopping sets were 56-footers, but the version with sliding luggage doors contained 58 ft composite coaches. In the 1930s at least three of the railmotor rebuilds worked on the branch:

Set No.	Coach No.
31	6559
32	5649
33	6557

The set numbers were soon painted out and the coaches then ran as normal 'loose' stock.

Pullman Holiday Coach No. P47 at Exmouth on 7th April, 1961 ready to be taken to Exton for the holiday season. Originally named *Rosalind*, it was built in 1921, withdrawn in 1960 for conversion to a Holiday Coach and by 1965 was in departmental use prior to preservation at Steamtown, Carnforth.

S.P. Derek

Ivatt class '2' 2-6-2T No. 41284 waits to leave Exmouth with the 6.50 pm train to Exeter Central, 26th August, 1962.

T.J. Edgington

Until 1951 the basic formation for Exeter-Exmouth services was a two-coach lavatory set coupled to a TL and a BCK, when the BCK was replaced by another TL. The loose thirds were of both the 56 ft and 58 ft types, including a rarer 58 ft type made from two six-wheel composite bodies on an SR underframe. The 56 ft coaches wore out first because their frames had not been renewed and were replaced by 58 ft composites from withdrawn 3-coach lavatory sets. With the expectation of heavier traffic in summer, all formations were increased, some trains being lengthened to no less than seven coaches consisting of a '2E-lav' set (the peculiar Exmouth half-corridor BTL-BCK sets, designated the 'E' type), three TLs or CLs and a two-coach lavatory set of any type. About 1953, push-pull sets Nos. 734 and 735, previously on the Plymouth to Turnchapel branch which had closed to passengers in 1951, were used as branch extras except when required as relief for the Seaton branch set. Each was composed of a CK and BTK converted from LSWR first class race special stock.

The 2-coach lavatory sets in the 1950s were green or carmine-red, sometimes both colours appearing in one set as the BCKs were always green with the exception of one crimson and cream Maunsell vehicle in Set No. 13. In 1955 the BCKs in Nos. 13 and 14 became life-expired and were replaced by Maunsell BCKs, only to be changed later in the year to LSWR BCKs. In 1956 the branch was supplied with carmine-red liveried Swindon-built 63 ft non-corridor coaches in 3-coach non-lavatory sets and loose seconds. These were the Southern's first new non-corridor steam-hauled coaches to be supplied for 30 years. Each set, capacity 32 first and 240 second class seats, was formed with brake second; first/second and brake second, with the set numbers painted at each end, as were the LSWR sets they replaced. They were repainted green by 1960.

Throughout the summer months and during rush hours all the year round, most of the Exeter-Exmouth trains consisted of five coaches, while at other times three or four sufficed. Apart from Lympstone which could only accommodate five coaches, other platforms could hold seven coaches which was the maximum at times of summer peak loading.

After the arrival of the new compartment stock, certain Exmouth branch services were required to be formed of corridor stock. Specific examples included the 8.10 am Exmouth to Exeter Central comprising two non-corridor seconds and a Bulleid corridor 3-set; the corridor section working through to Plymouth. These coaches had arrived at Exmouth on the previous day's 3.10 pm from Exeter Central. The two-coach Tipton St John's portion detached from the rear of the 5.18 pm Exeter Central after arrival at Exmouth was either a 2-lavatory set, or an ex-LSWR 10-compartment third (by now, re-designated 'second'), with Maunsell corridor brake composite, or later, after the disappearance of the LSWR stock from about 1960, a Maunsell corridor 2-set comprising a BCK with either a brake second, corridor second, or open second coach.

After the introduction of diesel multiple units on the East Devon branches from Monday 4th November, 1963, the few remaining steam-hauled services between Exeter, Sidmouth, Exmouth and Exeter still used the Maunsell sets. These and the newer compartment stock (the 3-coach sets and seconds built 1953-6 at Swindon) were all transferred to the Western Region during 1963, the visible alteration being the prefix 'S' altered to 'W'. In connection with the withdrawal of compartment stock for conversion into Carflats, WR corridor stock was scheduled to be substituted into some of the remaining steam workings from 3rd February, 1964, but this did not actually occur until mid-April.

On summer Saturdays, ex-LMS stock was used for through working to Manchester, while LMS stock was also part of the formation of an earlier commuter working to Exeter Central leaving at 8.21 am, the complete train of nine corridors having been previously worked down to Exmouth either as empty stock, or non-stop passenger service from Exeter Central. Even ex-LNER stock could be formed in the Manchester service, on occasion bringing the rare sight of a Gresley articulated twin-set.

Exton (formerly Woodbury Road) was host to one or two camping - later Pullman Holiday - coaches, from 1935 up to withdrawal of this facility by the Western Region at the conclusion of the 1964 summer season. They were worked to and from the station by the local freight. Ex-LSWR bogie stock was noted there in 1948 (No. S20), No. S14 in 1955, and in 1961 two Pullman Holiday coaches (Nos. P47 and P53), having been converted in 1960 from the 1921-built Pullman car *Rosalind*, and 1910-built car *Florence* respectively.

Glossary
  BCK Corridor Brake Composite
  BTK Corridor Brake Third
  BTL Non-corridor Brake Third (Lavatory)
  CK Corridor Composite
  CL Non-corridor Composite (Lavatory)
  TL Non-corridor Third (Lavatory)

Exmouth Junction: ex-LSWR coaches previously in use as Camping Coaches at East Devon sites, 18th September, 1965.   *R.A. Lumber*

EXETER AND EXMOUTH LINE.

Miles.		ON WEEK DAYS.							ON SUNDAYS.					
		a.m.	a.m.	Goods & Pass p.m.	p.m.	p.m.	p.m.	p.m.	a.m.	a.m.	p.m.	p.m.	p.m.	p.m.
	EXETER ....dep.	7 20	10 15	1 5	2 55	5 45	8 0	9 45	7 35	10 35	2 30	4 30	6 10	8 0
5½	Topsham	7 31	10 29	At 12.30 Up arr. 1 25	Arr. Up Gds. arr. 3 9	5 59	8 14	9 59	7 49	10 49	2 41	4 44	6 24	8 14
7	Woodbury Road	7 39	10 34	1 33	3 14	6 4	8 19	10 4	7 54	10 54	2 49	4 49	6 29	8 19
8½	Lympstone	7 44	10 39	1 40	3 19	6 9	8 24	10 9	7 59	10 59	2 54	4 54	6 34	8 24
10¾	**EXMOUTH** ....arr.	7 50	10 45	1 50	3 25	6 15	8 30	10 15	8 5	11 5	3 0	5 0	6 40	8 30

Miles.		ON WEEK DAYS.							ON SUNDAYS.					
		a.m.	a.m.	Goods & Pass p.m.	p.m.	p.m.	p.m.	p.m.	a.m.	p.m.	p.m.	p.m.	p.m.	p.m.
	EXMOUTH ......dep.	6 40	9 0	12 30	2 0	5 0	7 0	9 0	9 20	1 0	3 30	5 15	7 0	9 0
2¼	Lympstone	6 46	9 6	12 36	2 10	5 6	7 6	9 6	9 26	1 6	3 36	5 21	7 6	9 6
3½	Woodbury Road........	6 51	9 11	12 41	2 20	5 11	7 11	9 11	9 31	1 11	3 41	5 26	7 11	9 11
5½	Topsham	6 56	9 16	12 46	2 30	5 16	7 16	9 16	9 36	1 16	3 46	5 31	7 16	9 16
10¾	**EXETER** ....arr.	7 10	9 30	1 0	2 45	5 30	7 30	9 30	9 50	1 30	4 0	5 45	7 30	9 30

Exeter and Exmouth line timetable from 1st July, 1861.   *Author's Collection*

Topsham view looking in the down direction *c.* 1911. An 'O2' class 0-4-4T heads an up train. Boards cover point rodding in the 6 ft way.   *Author's Collection*

Chapter Eleven

Timetables

Exeter-Exmouth (Local Services)

The opening service from Exmouth to Exeter, Queen Street, which until 1976 was generally the terminus of branch trains, was five each way including Sundays. It was unusual to have an equally frequent Sunday service, though departure times were different from weekdays. Trains took 30 minutes for a distance of 10½ miles, stopping at all stations. From 1st July, 1861 the service was increased to seven each way and six on Sundays, but was reduced in November to six each way and four on Sundays. In June 1863 the winter service of six trains daily in each direction and four on Sundays increased to seven and five respectively. By August 1887 the service had further increased to ten down and eleven up trains, with five on Sundays, down trains taking from 29 to 31 minutes, times varying from 30 to 32 minutes for those in the up direction. By August 1905 a train ran non-stop leaving Exmouth at 9.30 am and arriving Queen Street at 9.48, a return service leaving Queen Street at 6.12 pm and arriving Exmouth at 6.30. From 1st June, 1908, in addition to the 18 trains each way between Exeter and Exmouth, a railmotor service was introduced between Exeter and Topsham making ten trips daily each way and five on Sundays.

In the summer of 1909 18 down and 19 up trains ran, with six each way on Sundays, taking 25 minutes in the down and 26 minutes in the up direction and stopping at the stations, but omitting the halts. This gave an approximate half-hourly service mornings in the up direction and in the early evening in the down direction. Additionally nine motor trains ran to and from Topsham stopping at the halts and took 17 minutes each way compared with the 12 minutes taken by the Exmouth trains running non-stop from Exeter to Topsham. Five motor trains ran on Sundays. The following April there were 18 down trains plus a late evening train on Wednesdays, Fridays and Saturdays; 16 up trains ran with the addition of a late train on the same evenings. One ran non-stop from Exmouth to Exeter in 18 minutes. The railmotor service remained unaltered.

In the summer of 1922 the LSWR offered a service of 17 trains each way with five on Sundays. With the demise of the steam railmotors the shuttle service to Topsham had ceased. The Southern Railway began well in the summer of 1923 with an improved service of 20 down and 21 up trains. In the summer of 1932 there were 22 down trains Mondays to Fridays, plus one additional on Wednesdays. The 7.48 am up was booked through to Plymouth, curiously running into Platform 1 Bay at Queen Street. The 8.20 pm ran through from Sidmouth Junction. On Saturdays there were 23 each way and on Sundays, 14 down and 15 up. Nine were scheduled to run each way on Sundays in the winter 1932-3. By 1935 the weekday morning 'express' was allowed 20 minutes and now served Topsham. In September 1937 27 trains ran in each direction and 19 on Sundays. A half-hourly service ran for part of the day, and these left Exeter or Exmouth at fifteen or forty-five minutes past the hour.

'M7' class 0-4-4T No. 35 approaching Polsloe Bridge Halt with a 5-coach Exmouth-Exeter Central train on 21st May, 1935.   *H.C. Casserley*

'M7' class 0-4-4T No. 30671 with a train for Exeter Central, arrives at Polsloe Bridge Halt on 22nd August, 1950.   *Wessex Collection, South Western Circle*

Before car ownership became almost universal, the Exmouth branch catered for many needs - commuters, students and schoolchildren, shopping trips, military, holidaymakers and excursionists. On sunny Sundays, short notice specials would be arranged by Exeter Control to clear the platforms of trippers bound for Exmouth in allotted 'Q' (as required) paths in the timetable, with similar arrangements for their return in the evening. They were nicknamed 'Sandhopper's Trains'. During pre-World War II summers 6d. return excursions were run every evening so that Exeter folk could get a breath of sea air and maybe have a swim. The price of the ticket gave rise to the excursion being nicknamed 'Woolworth's Special', that store selling goods at 3d. and 6d.

From 1st May, 1948 a special late train was run on Saturdays only to take dancers home from the Pavilion Ballroom, Exmouth, to Exeter or stations en route. Ballroom patrons showing the return half of their rail ticket were given a reduction on the three shillings admission ticket on entry. Although the regular departure was 11.45 pm, it subsequently became necessary to run it in two, or even more portions, in which case the first would depart at 11.45 and call at Topsham only, the second following at 11.52 and calling at all stations. Special extra late dance trains would be arranged on Bank Holidays Mondays and for the Christmas or New Year festivities when dancing would finish later than the customary 11.30 pm. In this event the line would be kept open for the special leaving as late as 12.45 am. Although from 1951 the train was lightly loaded during the winter months, 10 years later it was still the practice for the junior clerk in the Trains Office at Exeter Central district traffic superintendent's office to ring Exmouth station on Monday morning to record the 11.50 pm Dance Train passenger figures so that its existence could be justified. By the summer of 1963, although the working timetable included an 11.45 pm 'Q' path calling now at Polsloe Bridge Halt only, followed by an 11.57 'Q 'stopper', in practice only the one booked service, the 11.50 pm, ran. The two 'Q' paths were withdrawn after 7th September, 1963, but the late Saturday service survived until 5th May, 1968, to reappear at the earlier time of 11.23 pm from 4th May, 1971.

Returning to the 1948 service, that summer 23 down and 24 up trains ran on weekdays, with 13 each way on Sundays. In 1951 24 down trains ran Mondays to Fridays and winter Saturdays, with 26 on summer Saturdays, while the Sunday service was 13 each way in summer and 11 in winter. The up direction enjoyed a service of 25 trains on weekdays and winter Saturdays, with 27 on summer Saturdays. Trains were allowed about 26 minutes for the distance with a 30 second stop at the majority of stations though 1 minute was generally allowed at Topsham and 1 to 1½ minutes at Polsloe Bridge Halt, which is indicative of traffic at the latter. In the summer of 1957, 30 down trains ran, seven stopping at St James' Park Halt, one train running non-stop early on Saturday mornings only, from Exeter Central to Exmouth and a Mondays to Fridays lunch time train from Exeter to Topsham and back. Seventeen down trains ran on Sundays, six stopping at St James' Park Halt, plus a Polsloe Bridge Halt to Exmouth train to cope with the heavy tripper traffic originating there. Two trains omitted Woodbury Road and Lympstone. Thirty-one trains ran in the up direction, with the morning 'express', now 8.21 am, still calling at Topsham only and reaching Exeter in 21 minutes. Seven called at St James' Park Halt and one train ran to St

BR Standard class '3MT' 2-6-2T No. 82011 at Lympstone heading an Exmouth-Exeter Central train in August 1953.   *R.A. Lumber*

'M7' class 0-4-4T No. 30669 coasts into Woodbury Road station with the 10.45 am Exeter Central-Exmouth service on 4th September, 1958. From 15th September, 1958 this station was renamed Exton. The Exe estuary is on the left.   *H.B. Priestley*

David's on Saturdays only being the unadvertised through service to Manchester. Seventeen up trains ran on Sundays, six stopping at St James' Park and four omitting Lympstone and Woodbury Road. One omitted Topsham, but stopped at Polsloe Bridge and St James' Park. On 4th January, 1960 a non-stop evening express, the 5.45 pm Saturdays excepted, from Exeter Central to Exmouth was re-introduced taking 19 minutes for the run, one minute slower than in 1905, but accelerated to its old schedule from 14th June 1960. It was a popular train and gave keen drivers and good engines a brilliant opportunity to show their paces hauling a restricted load of four well-filled BR Standard non-corridor coaches. The punctuality of this service depended on the preceding 4.45 and 5.15 pm trains from Exeter Central, due Exmouth at 5.10 and 5.39 pm respectively. Immediately after their arrival, the 5.12 and the 5.40 pm departed from Exmouth. The latter was due at Topsham at 5.52 giving just enough time for the signalman to reset the road and cross the tracks to hand the tablet to the fireman of the express which passed at 5.54 or earlier, it not being unusual to arrive at Exmouth up to three minutes earlier than the booked time of 6.03 pm. After the engine had run round the coaches, the train called at Littleham and arrived at Budleigh Salterton at 6.25 pm. The re-introduction of this train was due to Charles Williams, divisional traffic superintendent at Exeter Central. He aimed to hold the substantial number of people who already travelled by train and also to win back from the roads some folk who were beginning to feel that road travel had its disadvantages. He was also largely responsible for the Cleethorpes to Exmouth service and in 1959 inaugurated a combined rail and coach tour of East Devon which gave facilities to London passengers to select the resort which most suited them.

On summer Saturdays in 1961 a train ran through to Yeoford on the Barnstaple line. The 14th June, 1963 was the last day of operation of the solitary lunch time train to Topsham, put on mainly for the benefit of workers at, or near, Exeter Central and was the remnant of the railmotor service. Topsham still had a very good service, being served by 61 trains daily. That summer there were 31 down trains (seven calling at St James' Park), including one with a through portion to Tipton St John's at 5.15 pm and the 5.45 pm non-stop Exeter Central to Exmouth which continued on after reversal to Budleigh Salterton. On Saturdays there were also 31 trains, seven calling at St James' Park. Seventeen down trains ran on Sundays (six calling at St James' Park and two omitting Exton and Lympstone), plus one from Polsloe Bridge to Exmouth. Thirty-one up trains ran on weekdays, including one through from Budleigh Salterton at 6.55 am (10 calling at St James' Park, while one train stopped at Topsham only). The 32 up trains on Saturdays included a through train to Yeoford at 9.54 am. Eleven trains called at St James' Park. Eighteen up trains ran on Sundays (nine stopped at St James' Park, four omitted Exton, three Lympstone and one Topsham). The branch was partially dieselised on 15th July, 1963 when diesel multiple units worked 12 trips each way, the first on the Budleigh branch being the 5.45 pm non-stop Exeter to Exmouth and thence to Budleigh. As dmus were required to stop at Topsham and Exmouth signal boxes for tablet exchange, the 5.45 actually ran nearly five minutes slower than its steam-hauled counterpart.

Most of the branch's services were dieselised on 9th September, 1963 and the winter timetable of 1963-4 saw the continuation of regular departures from Exeter

Central at 15 and 45 minutes past the hour, with some variations at peak hours but introducing off-peak reductions in the half-hour frequency. The schedules of some trains were reduced by two minutes, but in comparison with steam-hauled trains, the actual difference was hardly noticeable, being partly due to stopping at Exmouth signal box to exchange the tablet and partly to the fact that their steam predecessors had been covering the journey in less than the booked allowance, the timings being based on the performance of locomotives of the 'M7' class, rather than more modern types. Certain trains were diagrammed to work through to St David's and vice versa, through services to the WR main line being advertised, namely the 7.15 am Exmouth to Plymouth, 9.15 am to Kingswear and the 7.15 pm to Newton Abbot. The majority of trains were second class only. Twenty-seven ran in the down direction (seven stopping at St James' Park) and the non-stop to Exmouth, now scheduled a record 17 minutes, continued through to Budleigh Salterton. As an innovation, it additionally ran on Saturdays. Eleven ran down on Sundays, plus an additional six from 17th May, 1964. There were 29 up trains plus a late one on Saturdays, eight stopping at St James' Park and one stopping only at Topsham. Eleven trains ran on Sundays with an extra six running from 17th May. The Sunday train starting from Polsloe Bridge ceased.

The summer of 1964 brought a similar service with further through trains to Saltash, Ilfracombe, Paignton, Barnstaple Junction and Tiverton. Under Western Region administration which had taken over the branch on 1st January, 1963 more through trains ran than in the Southern era; though the through running of dmus was for convenience and economy of stock working, rather than providing a better service for passengers. Further changes took place with the commencement of the winter timetable on 7th September, 1964. Dmu diagrams were extended to cover longer journeys with minimum turn-round times at destinations. The intensive utilisation, together with maintenance problems, caused a marked increase in the number of delays and breakdowns. The 5.45 pm 'fast' commuters' train from Exeter was formed by the 3.45 pm ex-Ilfracombe which itself had arrived only 31 minutes previously direct from Salisbury (dep. 10.50 am) having originated from Yeovil at 7.30 am.

This journey length, combined with the long single line sections, contributed to late running, so much so that it became the practice to utilise the 5.49 pm steam engine and five WR coaches for the 5.45, thus ensuring a punctual departure and satisfied businessmen, while the late-running dmu covered the 5.49 pm stopping service. So steam once again ran non-stop to Exmouth after a lapse of nearly 15 months. At first, all five coaches were hauled to Budleigh, but subsequently, in view of the gradient, two were detached at Exmouth to lighten the load. The steam locomotive and coaches then continued working the diesel diagram until replaced by an available dmu. This 'Indian Summer' of steam working finally ceased from 4th January, 1965, when the 8.20 am from Exmouth and the 5.45 pm from Exeter Central were replaced by dmus, resulting from not only another revision of the dmu diagrams (to reduce their too intensive utilisation), but also the progressive elimination of steam from this new area of WR territory.

The winter of 1964-5 saw a reduction in the daily service with 25 down and 27 up trains running plus a late night one on Saturdays. Eleven Sunday trains each way were scheduled in September and May only, but the planned Sunday closure of the line from 4th October, 1964 to 25th April, 1965 as an economy measure was not implemented and the eleven trains continued to run. From 1st March, 1965 the 8.20 am up 'fast' called additionally at St James' Park. In the timetable for June 1965 to April 1966 the pattern was altered with more through trains to stations off the branch, yet in the locality. Twenty-eight down trains were shown, including one through to Tipton St John's; five from St David's; one to Budleigh Salterton and one from Ilfracombe. Twenty-six ran on summer Saturdays including three from St David's and 20 on summer Sundays, including one to Sidmouth and two from St David's which were the 10.10 am Plymouth and the 4.30 pm Goodrington Sands. Nine ran on winter Sundays, all but one running from St David's.

Twenty-eight up trains ran with the addition of a late one on Saturdays, five running to St David's; two from Budleigh Salterton, one from Sidmouth Junction and one from Sidmouth. On summer Saturdays there were 27 up, two running to St David's, the train arriving as the 8.12 am empty coaching stock from Exeter Central. On summer Sundays there were 27 up trains, including one from Sidmouth. Nine ran on Sundays in winter, all but two running through to St David's. On 18th April, 1966 Exmouth branch services were reduced to 26 trains each way, most noticeable withdrawals being the 8.22 am Exmouth to Exeter 'fast' and its return at 5.45 pm as a result of falling commuter traffic. On 3rd October, 1966, seven trains were withdrawn as an economy measure, six of them running between 9.00 am and 4.00 pm and 12 Saturday services were lost. Some lengthy 3¼ hour breaks in service further contributed to a fall in traffic.

In the timetable for March 1967 to May 1968 there were 23 down trains on summer weekdays (seven through from St David's and one from Honiton) and 21 up, of which five were through to St David's. On summer Saturdays there were 21 down (three from St David's) and 23 up. On winter weekdays only 19 ran (six through from St David's) and seven less on Saturdays. Eighteen up trains ran on winter weekdays (four through to St David's) with six less on Saturdays. Seventeen trains ran in each direction on summer Sundays, nine of these starting or terminating at St David's. In winter, all six served St David's. The service for the summer of 1968 was similar to that for the previous year, but for the first time, no less than ten ran through to St David's. No through trains ran to any other stations. The line's basic weekday service had dropped from 31 trains each way in 1963 to 19 in 1966, with 13 on winter Saturdays by 1968-9.

In the May 1969-70 timetable 20 trains ran each way on Mondays to Fridays with late afternoon/early evening services from 3.45 pm to 6.45 pm still remaining on the half-hourly pattern. A noteworthy feature was the reinstatement of the morning 'fast' to Exeter. In an attempt to reduce overcrowding on the previous year's 8.20 am from Exmouth, the morning pattern was altered to provide for an 8.01 am 'all stations' and an 8.29 am 'fast', the 28 minute interval being essential for the 8.01 to reach Topsham and cross the 8.00 from Exeter Central which arrived at Exmouth 8.25 to form the 8.29 am return, due Exeter Central 8.47. (From 1st May, 1972 the Exmouth departure became 8.30 and with the singling of the Topsham to Exmouth Junction section the token stop at Topsham was advertised in local publicity from 7th May, 1973 and in the WR timetable from 7th January, 1974, the train arriving Exeter Central 19 minutes after departure from Exmouth, before continuing to St

Topsham viewed on 15th April, 1986 with 'Pacer' No. 142 016 seen on a down train, *right*, and No. 142 074 on an up train. Note the bus-type shelter on the up platform beyond the original station building. The picture illustrates the problem caused by low platforms. A colour light signal is in position to replace the upper quadrant semaphore signal. *Stephen Cummins*

The 10.30 am Exmouth-Barnstaple service comprising class '108' Set 957 Nos. 51940/52057 north of Lympstone on 22nd July, 1989. Commando accommodation buildings are visible on the hill side in the background. *Author*

Set 871 made up of class '101' No. 53256 and class '108' No. 53639 working the 4.45 pm Exmouth-Exeter St David's service, climbing the 1 in 194 towards Lympstone on 21st July, 1989. *Author*

Car No. 52053 (right foreground) stands at Topsham with the 5.45 pm Exmouth-Paignton service, as Set 828 with the 5.48 pm Exeter Central-Exmouth train approaches on 3rd April, 1991.

Tom Heavyside

David's.) Twenty-five trains, including the 'fast', ran on summer Saturdays in 1969 and 16 in the winter. Twelve worked in each direction on summer Sundays and seven in the autumn and spring, none of the Sunday trains running through to St David's. This pattern of service continued. The most striking change was that there were no Sunday trains during the winter period 12th October, 1969 to 22nd March, 1970 and with no strong objections, this principle was adopted for successive years until requirements for Royal Marine traffic using Lympstone Commando station brought about a request for the winter Sunday service to be reinstated for 1978-79 which was acceded to after publication of the annual timetable, six trains running in each direction.

From 3rd May, 1976 all stopping trains served St James' Park and the newly opened Lympstone Commando which added one and two minutes respectively to the running time, increasing the overall schedule to 26 minutes in the down direction and to 27 minutes in the up. The morning 'fast' applied on all weekdays throughout the year and two through trains ran to and from Barnstaple. From May 1977 all Sunday trains and nearly all weekday trains went to and from St David's, with an additional two trains running through to Barnstaple. One advantage of through trains to Exmouth from stations off the branch was that rail passengers on a shopping trip from Barnstaple or Paignton to Exeter could ride through to Central, a station sited much more conveniently to shops than St David's, and they were not obliged to change trains at St David's, walk, or seek alternative transport. With the exception of the 8.30 am (times varied slightly) Exmouth to Exeter St David's 'fast' calling at Topsham only, all trains continued to call at all stations, with just five of the 20 Exmouth workings each way starting from or terminating at Exeter Central on weekdays. The overall pattern, however, remained at non-standard intervals, with off-peak gaps.

On Sundays from 12th October, 1980, special publicity was given to a new late night service at 11.10 pm from Exeter St David's to Exmouth, calling at Central, Topsham and Lympstone Commando only, with a return working departing Exmouth at 11.37 pm, calling at Lympstone Commando and Topsham only, to arrive at Exeter St David's at 12.01 am (Monday). The Summer 1981 timetable brought 23 workings each way Mondays to Fridays, one less on Saturdays, with four starting from or terminating at Exeter Central, but there were a minority of (mainly) off-peak workings omitting certain intermediate stations at variable intervals which could be a trap for the unwary. Consequently, the all-stations service was reinstated in the 17th May, 1982 timetable, with an approximately hourly pattern off-peak, and half-hourly at peak times when seven services started from Exeter Central and eight terminated there in the opposite direction. There was one through train from Paignton, and by the following year four ran through to Barnstaple Mondays to Fridays. From 14th May, 1984 in response to local pressure, a Lympstone stop was introduced in the 8.32 am Exmouth 'fast' which was frequently extended to Barnstaple in later years, but basically, the timetable remained unchanged until 12th May, 1986, when schedules were accelerated by approximately 3 minutes following introduction of the class '142' lightweight twin-set 'Pacer' dmus, and the number of trains was increased to 28 each way running at half-hourly intervals for most of the day, but five down and seven up off-peak services reverted to missing between one and four of the less-used intermediate stations, with resultant hourly frequency. Three workings started from Exeter Central and six in both directions served either Barnstaple, Newton Abbot or Paignton.

By the 16th May, 1988 timetable, services were again worked by the older 'Heritage' dmus brought in to replace the 'Pacers' which had been prematurely withdrawn the previous autumn, so schedules were decelerated by about three minutes to match the power, but overall, the timetable pattern and frequency remained virtually constant until 11th May, 1992 when a minority of Exmouth branch services were extended to and from Crediton as part of a Park and Ride local authority initiative to ease road traffic congestion in Exeter.

The winter timetable for 1993-4, based on an increased allocation of the new 'Sprinter' units, extended some workings to Milford Haven (!) and Gloucester for diagramming convenience, while the main feature was the introduction of a 'clock-face' timetable with the majority of departures from both Exeter Central and Exmouth timed to leave at 24 and 54 minutes past each hour, some trains taking as little as 20 minutes for the journey by omitting three or four stops, with Exton station a 'Request Stop'. All but two or three services in each direction were scheduled to call at the new Digby & Sowton station without detriment to the overall timing. In the event the station was not opened within the lifetime of that timetable.

The 1994 summer timetable showed 29 trains each way on weekdays, 27 on Saturdays and 13 on Sundays. On weekdays seven down trips originated from Barnstaple, five from Paignton, and one each from Cardiff Central, Newton Abbot and Plymouth. Of the up trains from Exmouth seven ran to Paignton, five to Barnstaple, and one each to Crediton, Newton Abbot and Carmarthen.

An innovation for summer Sundays, 1st June to 21st September, 1997 was the extension of selected Exmouth workings to and from the newly re-opened Okehampton station, (three down, one up), as part of an experimental tourist service of six trips each way between Exeter and Okehampton sponsored by various authorities to promote a public transport network linking with buses across Dartmoor. With the support of Camas Aggregates, owners of the normally freight-only line from the site of Coleford Junction through to Meldon Quarry, this enabled a regular passenger service to operate over this route for the first time since 1972.

Year	Day	No. of Trains Down (Exeter-Exmouth)	No. Serving St David's	No. Serving St James' Park
	Mon.-Fri.	32	0	7
1963	Summer Sats	31	1	7
	Summer Suns	18	0	6
	Mon.-Fri.	20	4	6
1969	Summer Sats	25	9	6
	Summer Suns	12	0	12
	Mon.-Fri.	20	17	20
1978	Summer Sats	23	17	23
	Summer Suns	11	11	11
	Mon.-Fri.	29	25	22
1994	Summer Sats	27	24	21
	Summer Suns	13	13	13

Main Line Through Services

Through coaches to and from Waterloo ran from at least as early as 1914 but as they travelled via Tipton St John's and Budleigh Salterton they are not relevant to this particular book, though one specially interesting train must be mentioned as it brought Eastern Region coaches to Exmouth on a regular basis. This was a Saturdays-only July to September Cleethorpes to Sidmouth and Exmouth train and a corresponding return working. Only started in 1960, it ceased running after September 1962 as a result of the Somerset & Dorset line being no longer used by through trains.

The only through train to use the Exmouth branch proper was the 9.22 am (later 9.18 am) summer Saturdays-only from Exmouth to Manchester which began running in 1949. The stock, usually 10 London Midland Region coaches, was taken to Exmouth each Monday evening and stabled there. On Saturday the train left in two parts: three or four coaches strengthening the regular branch set forming the 8.21 am Exmouth-Exeter Central, the remainder following an hour later. The latter were also hauled by a tank engine and on arrival at Exeter Central were coupled to those which had arrived earlier, a WR 4-6-0 locomotive, usually of the 'Hall' class, coming up from St David's to take the train onward. The Western Region refused to let the Southern region advertise it as a through train in case Exeter people bought their tickets at Central instead of St David's. Thus the SR public passenger timetable advertised the train as terminating at Central, while the WR publicised it as a St David's to Manchester through train via the Severn Tunnel. But despite the apparent confusion between the two Regions, it was known locally as a through Exmouth to Manchester service. In 1959 the SR advertised it as running through to St David's and from 1963, when the branch came under WR jurisdiction, the service was officially designated a through Exmouth to Manchester service. That year only, a corresponding 10.44 pm Fridays-only was run from Manchester to Exmouth. In its final year, 1967, departure from Exmouth was at 9.50 am and the following summer it became the 9.38 am from Newton Abbot.

In the late 1950s, arrangements were made for passengers for East Devon arriving at St David's after travelling overnight to be taken forward on summer Saturdays in coaches attached to a transfer fish and parcels train; this left St David's at 5.00 am for Central connecting there with a special running non-stop to Exmouth.

Diesel-hydraulic 'Warship' class No. D860 *Victorious* passing Polsloe Bridge Halt with the 9.50 am Exmouth-Manchester on Saturday 15th July, 1967.   *R.A. Lumber*

Chapter Twelve

Special Traffic Working and Freight Services

Special Traffic Working

In 1932 through excursions from Waterloo used the Exeter-Exmouth line on certain summer Sundays. For instance, the July 1935 Working Timetable included a 9.25 am National Sunday League excursion from Waterloo to Seaton and Exmouth via Exeter, returning at 6.20 pm; a 10.00 am Christchurch to Exmouth and Paignton; an 8.05 pm return excursion Bournemouth to Exmouth leaving Exeter Central at 11.23 pm and arriving Exmouth 11.48 pm, and finally an 8.40 pm return excursion Waterloo to Exmouth departing Exeter Central 12.55 am on Monday and arriving at Exmouth 1.20 am. Through excursions from Waterloo ran until 1964, though in their last year the Exmouth portion was detached at Sidmouth Junction and worked forward via Tipton St John's. Holiday Expresses (special trips from a town to a different destination for each day of a certain week), were run to Exmouth from WR stations such as Bridgwater, Bristol and Plymouth.

A 12.08 am pigeon special ran from Waterloo to Exmouth on some summer Saturdays conveying a maximum of nine bogies vans and a brake second, loaded with baskets containing pigeons which were released on arrival.

On Sunday 12th April, 1953 two specials were run in conjunction with two Ian Allan excursions from Waterloo. Class 'O2' 0-4-4T No. 30199 ran clockwise from Central to Sidmouth Junction, Tipton St John's, Exmouth and back to Central while Adams 4-4-2T No. 30583 completed the circuit anti-clockwise, the two trains meeting at Exmouth. On 1st September, 1954 Bertram Mills' Circus travelled in four special trains from Newton Abbot to Exmouth. The SR took over the trains from the WR at St David's, double-heading them throughout to Exmouth with 'M7' class 0-4-4Ts and BR Standard class '3' 2-6-2Ts with two bankers at the rear assisting on the gradient of 1 in 37 up to Central. Subsequently while the circus was performing in Exmouth three of the specials were berthed in Newcourt Sidings,* prior to their next working eastwards via the Budleigh Salterton branch. On 11th March, 1961 the 'Westward Television Exhibition Train' visited Exmouth, the three exhibition coaches being headed by Adams 4-4-2T No. 30582. On Sunday 2nd September, 1962 the Southern Counties Touring Society ran the 'South Western Limited' from Waterloo to Exeter via Exmouth, using 'M7' 0-4-4Ts Nos. 30025 and 30024 on the branch leg from Sidmouth Junction; while on Sunday 28th February, 1965 the Locomotive Club of Great Britain's East Devon railtour from Waterloo to Sidmouth and Exmouth had WR 0-6-0PT No. 4666, and Ivatt class '2' 2-6-2T No. 41206 working betweeen Tipton St John's and Exeter via Exmouth. This tour was repeated the following Sunday. The summer of 1964 saw a Sunday timetabled working by dmu from Tiverton to Exmouth and Sidmouth. Rolling stock arrived Tiverton at 9.10 am empty from Exmouth Junction, leaving 10 minutes later for its destinations. It returned only from Exmouth at 6.45 pm arriving Tiverton 8.07 pm, and leaving five minutes later, empty to St David's. The service finished on 6th September.

* S.C. Nash *Railway Observer*, January 1955.

'M7' class 0-4-4Ts Nos. 30024/5 leave Exmouth with an empty pigeon van special for Exeter, 2nd September, 1962.   *S.P. Derek*

'West Country' class 4-6-2 No. 34026 *Yes Tor* near Polsloe Bridge Halt with an up empty pigeon van train from Exmouth on 30th June, 1963.   *R.A. Lumber*

From 10th March, 1968 Exmouth had no facilities to deal with locomotive-hauled excursions as the removal of the run-round loop meant that no provision was made for getting a locomotive to the other end for the return journey. To overcome this difficulty, BR (WR) authorised the use of a second locomotive even though this was expensive in terms of power resources. On 10th May, 1969, a nine-coach excursion was organised by Exmouth School Association from Exmouth to Paddington and was probably the first locomotive-hauled passenger train to use the branch since the withdrawal of the Exmouth to Manchester service in September 1967. Following a successful test for the use of a class '47' diesel-electric locomotive over the branch on 8th April, 1970, the next excursion was run on 16th May, 1970 in connection with the naming ceremony of the *City of Birmingham* lifeboat at Exmouth Docks. An eleven-coach train from Birmingham, 'The Birmingham Post Special', was hauled throughout by Brush-Sulzer 2,750 hp class '47' No. 1700. At St David's the diesel-hydraulic 'Warship' class No. 811 *Daring* was attached to the rear and on arrival at Exmouth became the leading engine of the train which now formed the 12.45 pm booked passenger service back to Exeter. No. 1700 on the rear was detached at Exeter Central and the empty coaches drawn on for stabling at Exeter St David's. For the special's return journey the coaches formed the 5.45 pm Exeter Central to Exmouth booked passenger service hauled by No. 821 *Greyhound* with No. 1700 trailing, the latter becoming the train engine of the special which departed at 6.15 pm for Exeter Central (where No. 821 was detached) and Birmingham. As the excursion required the paths of the 12.02 pm from Exeter Central and 6.15 pm from Exmouth, these dmu services were cancelled, passengers using a special bus.

On 7th June, a 10-car dmu 'Pied Piper' excursion from Ealing ran to Exmouth via Basingstoke and Salisbury. This trip allowed children to travel free. On 20th June, Strong & Co. the brewers of Romsey, organised an outing to Exeter and Exmouth. From Romsey to Exeter Central the 11-coach special was double-headed by Crompton diesel-electric locomotives Nos. 6509 and 6505 and 2½ hours later, after the party had enjoyed luncheon at the Rougemont Hotel opposite the station, the special ran on to Exmouth in the 1.27 pm normal service path. No. 6509 led and 6505 trailed. The train then formed the booked 2.07 pm back to Exeter. For the return journey No 6505 hauled the regular 6.15 pm Exeter Central to Exmouth and the trailing engine No. 6509 then took the special to Exeter in the 6.45 normal service path, with 6505 now trailing. At Exeter Central No. 6509 ran round and re-coupled to 6505 and departed for Salisbury and Romsey. On each occasion the excursion ran in the normal service path; local passengers were also conveyed in addition to the excursionists.

During 1972 at least seven excursions were run to Exmouth, two of which were formed of engines and coaches. For example, on 28th May a 10-coach 'mystery' excursion came from Pembrey in Wales and on 25th June an 11-coach 'mystery' excursion arrived from Rhymney. The remainder were dmus from the London Division, that on 23rd July brought 10 cars comprising Sets L410 (4 cars), L458 and L473 (both 3 cars). On 3rd March, 1974 Hastings demus Nos. 1033 and 1035 made an appearance on a charter trip from Hastings. On 20th

Brush type '4' (class '47') No. 1638 on a return mystery excursion from Pembrey and Burry Port passing through Topsham on Sunday 28th May, 1972. Diesel-hydraulic locomotive No. 1013 *Western Ranger* is at the rear.   *R.A. Lumber*

A view of the rear of the train seen above with 'Western' class No. 1013 *Western Ranger* seen passing Topsham signal box, 28th May 1972.   *R.A. Lumber*

February, 1975 when there was a signalmen's strike in some areas and no through service could be run between Exeter and Salisbury, two class '101' dmu sets worked an 8.30 am special Exmouth-Exeter-Axminster-Exeter.

The additional expense caused by the need to have a locomotive at each end on the Exmouth branch caused a change in policy and the West of England Division declined to sanction any more after 1972. Then after a lapse of almost four years, locomotive-hauled excursions were, from May 1976, once again permitted. For instance, on 20th September, 1976 No. 25 080 worked the 7.58 am Exeter-Exmouth as a service train with No. 47 013 trailing. It returned as the 8.33 am Exmouth-Paddington Charter, working also as a service train to St David's. From 3rd June, 1977 'troop specials' of between 8 and 12 coaches have run from Lympstone Commando to various destinations and these continue to be a feature of the branch. Since 1994 HSTs tend to be used in order to avoid locomotives having to 'top and tail'.

The popular 'Santa Specials' introduced in 1985 during the weeks before Christmas, continue to raise considerable sums for charity, with staff donating money for surprise presents for children on board the train, specially decorated for the occasion with seasonal trimmings.

The Royal Train, conveying Prince Philip, ran to Lympstone Commando early in July 1993, while on 18th July, 1993 Hertfordshire Rail Tours' 'Atlantic Coast Express' ran from Waterloo to Barnstaple and Exmouth, hauled by class '50' No. 50 050 and 50 033 *Glorious* at the other end. This special marked the end of Network South East's locomotive-hauled operation on the Waterloo to Exeter route.

One special working was on the occasion of the Exeter Rail Fair held to commemorate the 150th anniversary of the opening of the Bristol & Exeter Railway to the city. On Sunday 1st May, 1994 the first steam locomotives on the Exmouth branch for 30 years took charge of the 11-coach 'Exmouth Venturer' special from St David's, but unfortunately the BR Standard class '4' 2-6-4Ts Nos. 80080 and 80079 heading and tailing the train stalled on the 1 in 37 gradient approaching Central station and arrival at Exmouth was an hour late. Although by then night had fallen, the train was welcomed by several hundred spectators.

A visit of a High Speed Train occurred on Friday 20th September, 1996, when the 'Exmouth Express' ran from Birmingham New Street conveying guests for the naming and dedication ceremony of Exmouth's new replacement lifeboat *Forward Birmingham*. The nine-vehicle formation included class '43' power car No. 43 071 leading, which before leaving Birmingham earlier that morning had been named *Forward Birmingham* (adorned with the RNLI crest). No. 43 080 was at the rear. Leaving Exeter St David's the special slotted into the booked path of the 11.51 am service train to Exmouth, on which local passengers were permitted, returning as the booked 12.24 pm. Later the HST again deputised for the local service train to Exmouth prior to forming the returning specials's departure at 4.24 pm.

One of the events during the Exeter Rail Fair held to commemorate the 150th anniversary of the opening of the Bristol & Exeter Railway, was the running of the first steam special on the Exmouth branch for 30 years. In gathering darkness, the delayed eleven coach 'Exmouth Venturer', with BR Standard class '4' 2-6-4Ts No. 80080 heading, and No. 80079 tailing the train, approach the terminus, 1st May, 1994. *S.P. Derek*

In connection with Exmouth's lifeboat renaming ceremony, the return working of the special HST from Birmingham to Exmouth (due 12.17 pm) formed the regular 12.24 pm public service departure back to Exeter St David's. The trailing power car (No. 43071) seen here, having earlier been named 'Forward Birmingham' (with RNLI crest), passes Topsham's redundant signal box with its 'TO LET' notice in the window on 20th September, 1996. No. 43080 is the leading power car of the 9-vehicle formation. *S.P. Derek*

Freight Services

In the early years of the century a down goods left Exeter at 8.10 am and shunted at stations and sidings *en route*, arriving at Exmouth 10.31. Wagons destined for Sidmouth were sent on behind an 'O2' which left at 10.45 am. The locomotives, usually an 0-6-0 double-framed Beyer goods which had brought the train from Exeter, shunted at Exmouth until the 'O2' returned from Sidmouth at 2.23 pm when the rest of the train could be made up ready for departure to Exeter at 2.52 pm, the city being reached at 5.23 pm. The (weekdays only) freight service in 1909 consisted of

7.10 am	Exeter-Exmouth, serving Topsham only.
10.45 am	Exeter-Exmouth, serving Western Counties & Collard's Siding; also Topsham Quay when required.
2.52 pm	Exmouth-Exeter.
4.07 pm	Engine and van, Topsham-Odam's Siding.
4.18 pm	Odam's Siding-Topsham.
5.00 pm	Exmouth-Exeter, serving Warren's Siding and Digby's Siding.

In 1932 the first down service from Exeter had become the 6.10 am from Exmouth Junction and the second, the 9.18 Exmouth Junction served Odam's Siding, but not Western Counties & Collard's. The engine and van continued to run. Return workings were at 2.40 pm serving Topsham Quay (it formed the working to Odam's Siding as it was at Topsham 3.17 to 5.01 pm) and Digby's Siding. The final up freight train left Exmouth at 10.10 pm. The year 1938 saw two additional workings: at 10.54 am from Exmouth Junction to Topsham, returning at 11.19, and 11.15 Exmouth to Topsham returning at 12.41 pm.

In the summer of 1951 the 6.05 am from Exmouth Junction Sidings ran non-stop to Exmouth arriving at 6.32. The 9.02 am shunted at all sidings *en route* arriving at 10.45. An additional 'Q' train ran at 10.15 am to Newcourt Sidings

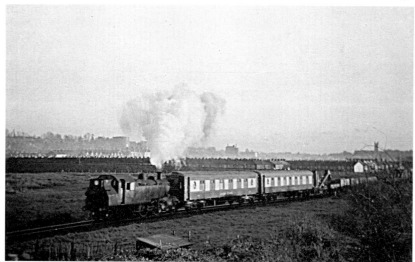

Exton's Holiday Coaches Nos. P53 and P47 leaving Exmouth on their way to Eastleigh via Exmouth Junction on the 3.45 pm freight, 2nd December, 1961 hauled by class '2MT' 2-6-2T No. 41318.

S.P. Derek

Ex-GWR 0-6-0PT No. 3759 on an up freight at Exmouth, 7th November, 1964. Notice the platform indicator on the signal post to warn the driver which side of the signal box he would pass to effect tablet delivery. *R.A. Lumber*

Exmouth-Exmouth Junction freight south of Topsham hauled by class '2MT' 2-6-2T No. 41307, 12th April, 1965. Freight working by steam ceased on 24th May, 1965. *R.A. Lumber*

returning at 11.27 and calling at Digby's Siding. There was one up freight (Exmouth dep. 3.16 pm) to Exmouth Junction Sidings (arr. 5.00 pm) shunting at all sidings except Newcourt. If it was required to shunt at Topsham Quay it omitted Digby's Siding. In 1963 one return working ran on weekdays Exmouth Junction to Exmouth departing at 5.47 am and leaving Exmouth at 3.50 pm. On Mondays, Wednesdays and Fridays an additional train left Exmouth Junction at 9.30 am, continuing to Tipton St John's at 11.08 am, this lasting until 24th January, 1964 when facilities were withdrawn from the Budleigh branch. The Newcourt working left at 12.10 pm, Saturdays excepted, returning at 2.10 pm. With steam's last duty on freight services ceasing on 24th May, 1965, the 5.45 am from Exmouth Junction Sidings and its return from Exmouth at 3.42 pm were amended to 10.55 am and 2.55 pm respectively. From 3rd January, 1966 freight services were revised as a result of the closure of Exmouth Junction Marshalling Yard. A 10.20 am Exeter Riverside ran to Exmouth on Mondays, Wednesdays and Fridays only, returning from Exmouth at 2.52 pm. Freight facilities on the branch were withdrawn as from 4th December, 1967 with the opening of the Coal Concentration Depot at Exmouth Junction, the Exmouth Dock branch was also closed from this date.

On 16th November, 1969, BR made a profit of £2,000 when it carried a hundred tons of machinery and equipment from Exton to Lympstone for Land, Sea & Marine Contractors of Cheshire in connection with the distribution of North Sea gas. This obviated the need for building a new road from Exton to the site. A 75 ton crane based at Swindon was given special authority to use the Exmouth branch where normally it was not permitted. In the 1970s Newcourt Sidings continued to be served by a mid-morning trip from Exeter Riverside running Mondays, Wednesdays and Fridays only when required and this ceased about 1986.

'Warship' class No. 858 *Valorous* on bridge No. 15, Exton, on Sunday 16th November, 1969 with Swindon 75-ton crane, on the occasion of laying a North Sea gas main across the river bed.   *R.A. Lumber*

Appendix One

Station Statistics

	Topsham			Woodbury Road			Lympstone			Exmouth		
	1928	1932	1936	1928	1932	1936	1928	1932	1936	1928	1932	1936
No. of passenger tickets issued	87,397	60,336	51,159	15,652	9,709	7,594	43,965	37,113	33,358	181,024	125,765	116,418
No. of tickets collected	100,595	70,576	63,984	21,522	13,775	8,340	45,048	46,951	45,048	434,362	296,734	294,690
No. of season tickets issued	848	839	973	112	127	184	309	304	455	1,699	2,490	2,555
No. of platform tickets issued	1,609	411	171	54	1	2	32	10	14	26,769	17,595	15,959
Parcels forwarded	5,257	4,161	3,472	930	601	1,245	939	1,082	1,122	8,499	7,264	6,675
Parcels received	3,788	3,732	4,447	967	1,243	1,279	1,032	1,313	1,758	30,768	28,702	33,240
Horses forwarded	1	3	3	-	-	-	1	-	2	60	11	45
Horses received	-	8	5	-	-	-	1	3	1	41	10	32
Milk forwarded (churns 1928, gallons 1932 & 1936)	-	-	-	972	2,325	2,715	-	-	4,061	2	933	-
Milk received (churns 1928, gallons 1932 & 1936)	-	-	-	11	-	-	-	-	10	2,623	13,443	2,771
General merchandise forwarded (tons)	2,713	1,749	1,141	229	82	110	128	69	67	10,572	17,958	8,111
General merchandise received (tons)	2,294	1,845	1,306	704	592	194	659	375	248	9,018	8,020	7,328
Coal, coke, patent fuel, forwarded (tons)	71	32	-	-	-	-	-	-	-	120	14	18,137
Coal, coke, patent fuel, received (tons)	7,661	8,473	8,826	598	895	884	838	840	676	22,025	19,613	8,354
Other minerals, forwarded (tons)	5,196	1,760	3,009	-	-	30	-	-	-	11,459	4,077	4,390
Other minerals, received (tons)	7,525	2,048	4,700	2,420	127	-	143	10	4	5,249	1,269	359
Livestock forwarded (No. of trucks)	51	-	4	-	-	-	25	2	2	-	-	1
Livestock received (No. of trucks)	42	27	42	-	-	-	31	3	2	3	1	-

Notes: Camping coach at Woodbury Road from 1935.

In 1933 a new fuel unloading plant was installed at Exmouth Docks.

Appendix Two

Facts from Questionnaire sent to each Household by Lympstone Parish Council (1989)

	Use of Local Bus Service		Use of Local Train Service	
	No.	%	No.	%
Daily	21	4	46	8
Weekly	34	6	82	15
Monthly	6	1	21	4
Sometimes	147	27	276	50
Never	318	58	96	18

Acknowledgements

Grateful acknowledgements for assistance is due to M.J.B. Blackstone; J..R. Bonser; I.G. Cann; W.G. Clarke; M. Daly; M.E.J. Deane; Devon Dock Dock, Pier & Steamship Co Ltd; Devon Record Office; L.L.G. Dolling; T.J. Edgington; Exmouth Library; W. Gorfin; S. Hawkins; T. Heavyside; W.H. Hoare; J.J. Herd; Miss M.M. Love; R.A. Lumber; S. Murch; S.C. Nash; Mrs G.L. Parkinson; C.M. Parsons; H.B. Priestley, G. Pridmore; R.C. Riley; R. Salway; D.R. Steggles; J. Stuart; Topsham Museum; D. Tozer; P.K. Tunks; R.J. Vince; A.L. Waggett; Mrs N.A. West; W.P. West, R. White and E. Youldon.

Special thanks must go to Dr T.R.N. Edwards for checking and improving the manuscript, as did S.P. Derek who, once again, placed a substantial amount of additional information at my disposal.

Exeter Central: the down bay platform used by some Exmouth trains. The sand drag is 18 inches deep and red lights are situated in front of the stop block, 19th July, 1989.

Author

Bibliography

Acts of Parliament
Antell, R., *Southern Country Stations No. 1*; Ian Allan (1984)
Boyle, V.C. & Payne D., *Devon Harbours*; Johnson (1952)
Bradley, D.L., *Locomotives of the LSWR*; RCTS (1967)
Bradley, D.L., *LSWR Locomotives, The Adams Classes*; Wild Swan (1985)
Bradley, D.L., *LSWR Locomotives, The Drummond Classes*; Wild Swan (1986)
Bradshaw's Manual 1869
Bradshaw's Railway Guides
Bush, R.J.E., *The Book of Exmouth*; Barracuda (1978)
Cann, I.G. & Bush, R.J.E., *Exmouth History*; Authors - typescript only
Casserley, H.C., *London & South Western Railway Locomotives*; Ian Allan (1971)
Clinker, C.R., *Closed Stations & Goods Depots*; Avon Anglia (1978)
Darwin, B., *War on the Line*; Southern Railway (1946, reprinted Middleton Press 1984)
Delderfield, E.R., *Exmouth Milestones*; ERD Publications (1948)
Delderfield, E.R., *Exmouth Yesterdays*; Raleigh Press (1952)
Hadfield, C., *The Canals of South West England*; David & Charles (1967)
Hateley, R., *Industrial Locomotives of South Western England*; Industrial Railway Society (1977)
Hawkins, C. & Reeve, G., *An Historical Survey of Southern Sheds*; Oxford Publishing Co. (1979)
Hawkins, C. & Reeve, G., *Southern Nouveau No. 1*; Wild Swan (1987)
Owen, J., *The Exe Valley Railway*; Kingfisher (1985)
Pryer, G.A., *Track Layout Diagrams of the Southern Railway & BR SR Section 5*; R.A. Cooke (1982)
Sekon, G.A., *The London & South Western Railway*; London (1896)
Thomas, D. St J., *Regional History of the Railways of Great Britain, No. 1 The West Country*; David & Charles (1981)
Williams, R.A., *The London & South Western Railway Vols 1 & 2*; David & Charles (1968 & 1973)

[The author was unable to trace the Exeter & Exmouth Railway Minute Books.]

Magazines: *British Railway Journal*; *Engineering*; *Illustrated London News*; *Railway Magazine*; *Railway Observer*; *Trains Illustrated.*

Newspapers: *The Alfred*; *Evening Post* (Exeter); *Express & Echo* (Exeter); *Exmouth Chronicle*; *Exmouth Journal*; *Exeter Flying Post*; *Western Luminary*; *Western Morning News*; *Woolmer's Exeter & Plymouth Gazette.*